Operations Pro

A Path to Success for Educational Institutions

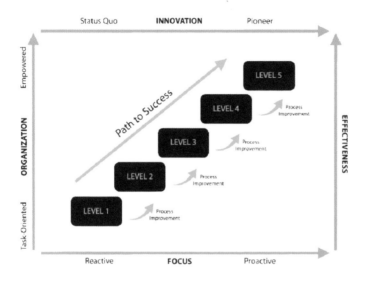

Jack Spain

SCHOOLDUDe

www.schooldude.com/opm

Operations Proficiency Model – *A Path to Success for Educational Institutions*

Publisher: **SchoolDude.com, Inc.**
Cover Design: **Jack Spain, SchoolDude and**
                Chris Duke, The WYSIWYG Group,
                http://www.TheWYSIWYGGroup.com

© 2013 **SchoolDude.com, Inc.**

2nd Edition – August 2013

    ISBN 978-0-615-79875-2
    1. Operations Proficiency Model.
    2. Performance Management. 3. Schools. 4. Higher Education.
    5. Maintenance Management. 6. Facilities Management.
    7. Energy Management. 8. Technology Management.
    9. Facility Usage. 10. Maturity Models.

This book is dedicated to all of the educational operations professionals that have devoted their lives to provide a comfortable, reliable, safe, clean, healthy, and technology-enabled learning environment for the future leaders of tomorrow.

SchoolDude.com
Cary, NC USA
jack.spain <at> schooldude.com
http://www.schooldude.com/opm

Table of Contents

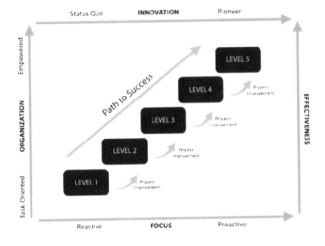

Preface

"If you're not keeping score, you're only practicing."
— Vince Lombardi

This book is targeted for educational professionals in public and private K-12 schools and colleges and universities who play a leadership role in the maintenance, support, and operations for their institutions. Whether the reader is in a senior administrative role or serves as a line manager for a facilities or technology team, our research was specifically inspired by leaders who make a passionate and selfless commitment to delivering exceptional education experiences through a high quality educational environment for their students every day.

We initiated our research with an appreciation and empathy that your organization is most likely already ***over-worked***, ***under-staffed***, and ***under-funded***. Within this context, we anticipate there are several valid questions to begin this discussion, along the lines of:

❒ Why should I invest time that I do not have to measure my organization's performance?

❒ What value will my organization receive in exchange for the effort required to implement an operational performance management program (i.e. show me my Return on Investment)?

❒ How much effort is required to implement performance management for my organization?

First of all, it is important to frame this discussion in the context that your students are constantly being measured on their achievements and test scores; and teachers and schools are currently being measured and held accountable to standards such as *No Child Left Behind* (NCLB)[1] and the *Common Core State Standards*[2]; faculty members are being graded on-line by students; and the performance of higher education institutions is constantly benchmarked against peer organizations in this country as well as globally.

Operations professionals supporting educational facilities play a mission critical role in educating our children that includes ensuring high quality, clean, safe, comfortable, healthy, appealing, and reliable classrooms with high quality technology, acoustics, and indoor air quality that are optimized for learning and student performance – along with a safe, secure, functional, and attractive surrounding environment. While energy, maintenance, and technology costs are a key focus for education leaders, the efforts from facilities, maintenance, custodial, energy, and technology staff members is apparent each and every day.

It is certainly a topic for debate on why you would want to promote change in your organization at the same time you are already overwhelmed with your current workload. We suspect you are already facing more challenges than you believe you can deal with most days with no relief in sight. Following are several points to reflect upon that provide a frame of reference on why we believe it is imperative that you commit to proactively managing the performance of your organization.

[1] http://www2.ed.gov/nclb/landing.jhtml
[2] http://www.corestandards.org/

1. Your stakeholders at large (students, parents, community, faculty, staff, administrators, vendors, etc.) continue to have higher expectations and demand more from their service providers each and every day.

2. Regardless to what degree we are wired to resist change – change is constant, and the rate of change continues to accelerate.

3. Well-conceived and planned performance management programs provide a consistent method to recognize and reward your staff members for a job well done and can be a positive factor in minimizing unplanned staff turnover.

4. A proactive program to measure and monitor your organization provides you with very objective metrics that you can leverage to negotiate for financial and human resources to support your operation.

We also recognize that the education sector is facing serious challenges today, and we have witnessed what we believe has emerged as a *"Perfect Storm"* for educational institutions over the past decade. Public K-12 schools have experienced a crescendo of challenges that have been developing over the past several decades. We have highlighted some of the critical challenges in the following diagram.

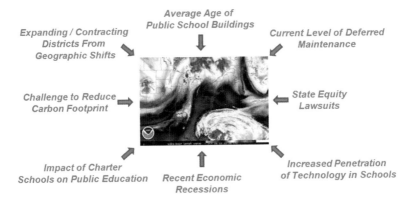

Figure 1 – The "Perfect Storm" for Schools [3]

We suspect that many private K-12 schools are also facing similar challenges with regard to budgets, deferred maintenance backlogs, and technology penetration. It becomes even more daunting when you factor in increased expectations from parents that they are receiving a positive return on their investment in their child's education.

[3] http://www.ssd.noaa.gov/goes/east/eaus/wv.jpg

We believe that a *"Perfect Storm"* for higher education institutions has also been brewing for quite some time and is headed towards a Category 5 status based on the factors highlighted in the following diagram.

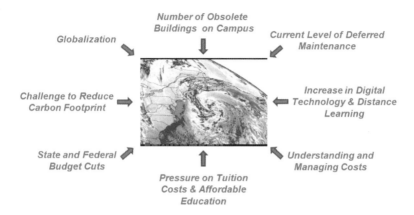

Figure 2 – The "Perfect Storm" for Colleges and Universities [4]

We decided to focus on performance management as a proactive defensive mechanism to brace and persevere against the challenges described above. Our model and methodology is by no means a magic wand to eradicate the challenges that you are facing, but we certainly do believe it provides a very pragmatic approach to position your organization to succeed in the face of adversity.

We define **operations performance management** as a process to measure progress and results toward the goals of your organization with the objective of identifying continuous process improvement initiatives to increase and enhance your organization's ability to execute. We believe

---

[4] http://chronicle.com/article/A-Perfect-Storm-in/126451/

that a well-defined and properly implemented operations performance management program is an exceptional vehicle to translate *subjective* vision, mission, and value statements into clearly defined *objectives*. We believe that it:

1. Is a vehicle to align detailed organizational objectives with strategic enterprise goals;
2. Is a method to simplify communicating strategic goals and supporting objectives;
3. Is a technique to communicate using specific objective metrics versus subjective ideas;
4. Is a tool to successfully set and manage expectations for your internal customers, staff, and management;
5. Is an efficient method to keep your management and administration informed on the performance and results delivered by your organization;
6. Is a means to attain transparency, visibility, and integrity across your organization;
7. Is a method to align your human and financial resources in your organization toward common outcomes;
8. Is a technique to align your staff with the enterprise goals;
9. Is a tool to position you to be proactive in addressing potential issues and shortcomings;
10. Is a vehicle to prioritize key initiatives and focus your staff on the right initiatives at the right time;
11. Is a means to improve your organization's ability to execute efficiently and consistently while reducing variability in your overall performance;
12. Is an approach to promote informed decision-making;
13. Is a strategic asset to keep your organization moving in a positive direction from your continuous improvement initiatives;
14. Is a process to measure progress in achieving goals and objectives;

15. Is a method to create uniformity in how things are measured in your organization.

We do not anticipate that we will energize your organization to define 50,000 points of data to analyze on a routine basis like Alaska Airlines[5], but we certainly aspire to encourage you to re-evaluate your current performance management programs and tools and consider our model as a catalyst for improving your organization's performance – cultivating a culture that embraces continuous improvement.

We delve into responses for the why, what, how much, etc. for operations performance management initiatives in more detail in the next section.

---

[5] http://www.nytimes.com/2013/03/03/business/alaska-airlines-flying-above-an-industrys-troubles.html?pagewanted=all&_r=0

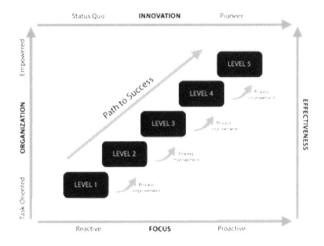

Operations Impact on Student Performance

"Let your performance do the thinking."
– H. Jackson Brown Jr.

The **Operations Proficiency Model (OPM)** is a *Path to Success* for leaders who are accountable for providing operational support for educational facilities. The quality of the operational environment of a school facility is paramount to cognitive functioning and overall student performance. Critical elements include:

- Clean **Indoor Air Quality** is fundamental to student and instructor health
- Consistent **Thermal Comfort** is critical for concentration
- Safe environments for **physical activity** impact student health and engagement
- Classroom **Lighting** is essential for a functional, clear visual experience
- Quality **Acoustics** are fundamental to listening
- Proven security systems, policies, and procedures to ensure student and staff **Safety**
- Functioning **Technology Assets** have a direct impact on learning
- Cost savings from **Energy Conservation** efforts fund new curriculum tools and materials

The *Center for Green Schools*[6] recently published excellent research connecting school facilities with student health,

---

[6] http://www.centerforgreenschools.org/

titled *"The Impact of School Buildings on Student Health and Performance"*[7]. This research highlighted the correlation of school design and construction, operations and maintenance practices, and other human variables with student learning. These environmental factors can play a dramatic role in student performance. The *National Clearinghouse for Educational Facilities* has compiled an excellent list of resources on the *"Impact of School Facilities on Learning"* [8].

Educational technology is pervasive and fundamental to learning in all schools and campuses today. The number of devices that each operation has to manage and integrate continues to increase every year, simultaneous to an ever decreasing life cycle of hardware and software technologies. Technology is also becoming increasingly more fundamental to measuring student performance, including the *Common Core Standards*[9].

While many "operational" functions are performed as assigned in the background and far too often receive little to no visibility – each of the factors noted above has a direct impact on attendance, student performance, and staff engagement. Sound operational planning and performance pave a *Path to Success* for educator and student performance.

---

[7] http://centerforgreenschools.org/Libraries/Publications/McGrawHill_ImpactOnHealth.sflb.ashx?
[8] http://www.ncef.org/rl/impact_learning.cfm
[9] http://www.parcconline.org/sites/parcc/files/PARCCTechnologyGuidelines2dot1_Feb2013Update.pdf

Background on Performance Management

"We wanted to talk about quality, improvement tools, and which programs work. He wanted to talk to us about management, cultural change, and senior managers' vision for the company."
– A Ford executive in 1990, regarding a consultation with W. Edwards Deming.[10]

There is an incredible wealth of resources and best practices available from the past century regarding quality, productivity, process improvement, and performance management. Many of the processes that organizations have implemented over the past few decades incorporate a blend of the methodologies that were developed in the AT&T Western Electric Plant back in the early to mid-1900s, then refined throughout Japan after World War II, and subsequently adopted and refined in corporations throughout North America. We embrace the performance management pioneers including Shewhart, Duran, Deming, Ohno, Crosby, Juran, Imai, Humphrey, Smith, Kaplan, Norton, and Nakajim to highlight just a few.

The **Operations Proficiency Model** was designed as a *performance measurement* framework to facilitate the identification of performance measures that contribute to the identification of *continuous improvement* initiatives for organizations responsible for maintaining and operating **schools** and **college campuses**. The OPM can be used as a guide to record and monitor the results of your quality management initiatives, process optimization and continuous process improvement efforts, and business performance management programs. The model positions your organization to communicate

---

[10] Swift, J. A., Vincent K. Omachonu, and Joel E. Ross. "Strategic Quality Planning." *Principles of Total Quality.* 2nd ed. Boca Raton, Fla.: St. Lucie Press, 1998. 59.

the results of your actions with "data" and ideally creates a story that is credible and "speaks for itself".

The overarching goal of this model is to provide educational leaders with tools to effectively:

- **Align** institutional, departmental, and individual **goals**
- **Communicate** effectively with "objective" data and actual results
- Deliver **visibility** and **transparency** for critical organizational results
- Facilitate **prioritization** of resources and initiatives
- Provide a catalyst for identifying **continuous improvement** initiatives

We believe that the tools, best practices, and insights that we share in this book provide the foundation for a *Path to Success* for operational leaders and executives supporting educational institutions. While this book is focused on providing you with insights on how to implement an effective performance management process for your organization, we have also included additional background information on quality, performance management, measurement, and benchmarking in the *Brief History of Performance Management* section toward the end of this book.

Introduction to the OPM

"What's measured improves."
— Peter F. Drucker

What is the Operations Proficiency Model?

The Operations Proficiency Model (OPM) is a *performance measurement model* specifically developed as a framework to enable the identification of performance measures that facilitate identification of *continuous improvement* initiatives for organizations responsible for maintaining and operating schools and higher education institutions.

The **Operations Proficiency Model Is** NOT:

- An academic exercise
- Designed as a comprehensive model to cover maintenance and operations across all industries including commercial real estate, industrial, and manufacturing *(where the majority of industry research has been conducted)*
- Designed from a computer system or software product perspective *(i.e. CMMS, EAM, ERP, ITAM, etc.)*

The **Operations Proficiency Model Is:**

- A **pragmatic** and **comprehensive** model to illuminate a *"Path to Success"* for operations organizations
- Targeted specifically for **facilities, maintenance, energy,** and **technology** (IT) services organizations that support *schools* and *higher education* institutions

While numerous traditional financial measurements exist for virtually all industries, we have found limited sources of models and frameworks for measuring operational performance specifically for educational institutions.

Why did we develop a new Model?

SchoolDude initiated an investigation in the second half of 2012 for an accepted **industry standard** *performance,* *maturity, or* **capability** **model** for Facilities and Maintenance Management to incorporate as a strategic element and underpinning of their new **Success** **Plus** services offerings. While research has been conducted towards defining *Key Performance Indicators* (KPIs) for maintenance; our investigation failed to uncover a pragmatic process improvement model and set of guidelines for operations for educational institutions *(Maintenance, Facility Usage, Energy, Technology).*

SchoolDude has decades of experience in developing solutions to support the dedicated personnel that support schools and campuses throughout North America. We have designed, developed, and delivered a comprehensive suite of operational maintenance, energy, and technology management solutions for the education sector since 2001. Since that time we currently host the most extensive database of maintenance, facilities, energy, and technology-related data for schools and campuses in the nation in our cloud-based Software as a Service (SaaS) suite of applications. Over the past decade we have assembled a team of professionals that now includes thousands of years of experience supporting education facilities.

In concert with our commitment to position educational operations professionals with best-in-class tools and techniques, we decided to conduct research on the current industry best practices and combine that with our industry expertise to develop a roadmap for our clients to embrace performance management and continuous improvement to support their institution.

We believe that SchoolDude is uniquely positioned today to continue to play a very strategic leadership role for operating schools and campuses throughout North America and we have committed to evangelizing the **Operations Proficiency Model** to assist our clients in reaching their goals and objectives for operating educational institutions across the nation.

Where is the OPM applicable?

The **Operations Proficiency Model** has been specifically designed for professionals who have operational responsibilities and accountabilities to support **K-12 schools** and **college and university campuses**. Typically this would be professionals that work in a business office or the facilities, maintenance, energy, and technology departments.

Who are the target beneficiaries for the OPM?

We believe that any professional directly or indirectly involved in administering, managing, supporting, or delivering operational services for schools or higher education institutions can benefit from establishing and monitoring performance metrics. Specific positions and roles include:

- College and University Chancellors

- College and University Vice Chancellors
- College and University Presidents
- College and University Vice Presidents
- School Business Officers
- School Superintendents
- School Chief Financial Officers
- School Assistant Superintendents
- State Education Officials
- School Board Members
- School and Campus Maintenance and Facilities Vice Presidents
- School and Campus Maintenance and Facilities Directors
- School and Campus Maintenance and Facilities Managers
- School and Campus Maintenance and Facilities Supervisors
- School and Campus Maintenance Technicians
- School and Campus Energy and Utility Managers
- School and Campus Energy Efficiency Program Managers
- School and Campus Chief Information Officers
- Information Technology / Technology Services Vice Presidents
- Information Technology / Technology Services Managers
- Information Technology / Technology Services Supervisors
- Information Technology / Technology Services Technicians

How Much effort is required to use the OPM?

We anticipate that the requirements and expectations will be unique for each organization that commits to plan, design, develop, and maintain their customized and personalized version of the **Operations Proficiency Model.** Identifying the specific **performance characteristics** and **key performance indicators** will likely be the most straight-forward element of the equation and will *not* require substantial resources. Quite often the challenges with this type of program include effective *communications; change management; empowering* and *inspiring* your entire staff to embrace and engage in *performance management* and **continuous process improvement**; and ultimately instilling *accountability* for the metrics across the organization.

How do we implement the OPM for our school or campus?

The most critical factor to understand is that implementing a performance management program, like the **Operations Proficiency Model**, is a **process**, *not* a sporadic *event (i.e. when it is convenient)*. As true with many initiatives, your organization will ultimately derive more benefits from the process, than capturing and analyzing specific numbers.

We anticipate that some organizations will begin in one specific area or discipline and expand to others over time. Other organizations will choose to focus on all operational disciplines simultaneously. It is acceptable to start small, build sustainable processes, confidence, and support across your organization before making a more significant commitment. It is also acceptable to initially design and implement a comprehensive program that encompasses all disciplines with a long-term perspective on what you ultimately want to achieve.

There is not a right or wrong approach as long as you can clearly demonstrate that you are making progress towards identifying the relevant measures for your organization; making the appropriate decisions based on the data and trends you are monitoring; and making tangible process on operational continuous process improvement across your organization. You will identify new critical and strategic metrics to monitor and discover others are no longer as important as they were previously. It is essential to also consider OPM as a *continuous process improvement* initiative for your organization.

When should we consider adopting the OPM?

Today, obviously!

The sooner you begin to identify and capture metrics *(results)* on a consistent basis, the sooner you can begin to monitor trends and make informed decisions to improve your operations. The process should not be dependent on your annual school or fiscal calendar. It will be in your best interest to begin capturing relevant metrics as quickly as feasible to support your subsequent analysis, decision-making, and future continuous improvement initiatives.

A Secret Ingredient

Performance management initiatives are most successful when your senior leaders and top management are committed and engaged with the process. Initially you must be able to identify "common ground" through clearly connecting the efforts and results of your organization with the goals and objectives of your institution. Once you have made this correlation, it may likely present you with another challenge to proactively manage expectations and ensure that your key stakeholders have a realistic understanding on what can be achieved in what timeframe. Ideally you should aspire to have a consistent message and steadfast support from the top to the bottom of your organization.

Overview of the OPM

"The greater danger for most of us lies not in setting our aim too high and falling short; but in setting our aim too low, and achieving our mark."
— Michelangelo

The **Operations Proficiency Model** is comprised of several components or views, which include:

a. **Five** (5) **Levels** that indicate operational *maturity*.

Each progressive **Level** is in recognition of an increasing level of proficiency and operational maturity. We have designated these levels as follows:

1. Level 1 ....Manual
2. Level 2 ....Automated
3. Level 3 ....Disciplined
4. Level 4 ....Measured
5. Level 5 ....Distinguished

b. **Four** (4) functional **Disciplines**.

The functional **Disciplines** that we have defined incorporate the key operational responsibilities for supporting schools and campuses, including:

1. Maintenance Management
2. Facility Usage
3. Energy Management
4. Technology Management

c. **Five** (5) leadership **Dimensions**.

Each of the proficiency Levels includes a series of leadership **Dimensions** that further characterize the operational maturity of the organization. We have defined these Dimensions as:

1. **Organization**
2. **Process**
3. **Technology**
4. **Planning**
5. **Measurement**

d. *Dozens* of **Performance Characteristics** associated with each Level and Discipline.

We have created a series of illustrative **Performance Characteristics** as a guide for determining the Level of performance for each Discipline within the OPM.

e. *Dozens* of **Key Performance Indicators (KPIs)** associated with each Level and Discipline.

One of the key goals in developing the **Operations Proficiency Model** is to provide a library of relevant Key Performance Indicators that can be used as a template to monitor performance and performance trends that are critical for your institution and to leverage them as a catalyst for continuous process improvement initiatives throughout the organization.

OPM Maturity Levels

"Successful and unsuccessful people do not vary greatly in their abilities. They vary in their desires to reach their potential."
– John Maxwell

The **OPM** Maturity Levels have been developed as a designation of the maturity and capabilities of an operations organization supporting schools and campuses. We have included a graphical representation of the **Operations Proficiency Model Maturity Levels** below.

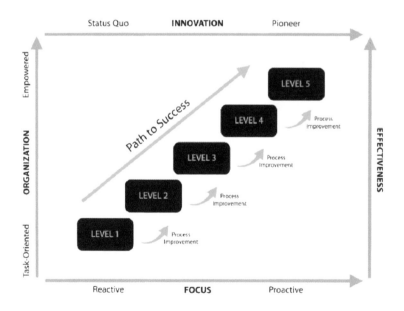

Figure 3 – OPM Maturity Levels

This diagram illustrates the progress that an organization makes along the lines of ***staff empowerment, innovation, strategic focus***, and ***overall effectiveness*** as it takes on increasingly more progressive and advanced Performance Characteristics. One perspective is to look at a progression from a Level 1 state of the "building *(or your workload)* is managing you" to a Level 5 state where you are clearly "managing the building".

The next chart provides a high-level description of each of the **OPM** maturity levels.

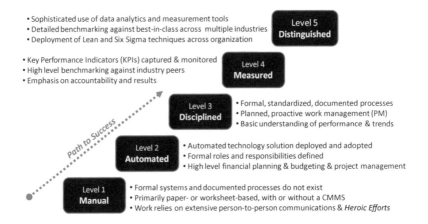

• Sophisticated use of data analytics and measurement tools
• Detailed benchmarking against best-in-class across multiple industries
• Deployment of Lean and Six Sigma techniques across organization

Level 5 Distinguished

• Key Performance Indicators (KPIs) captured & monitored
• High level benchmarking against industry peers
• Emphasis on accountability and results

Level 4 Measured

Level 3 Disciplined
• Formal, standardized, documented processes
• Planned, proactive work management (PM)
• Basic understanding of performance & trends

Level 2 Automated
• Automated technology solution deployed and adopted
• Formal roles and responsibilities defined
• High level financial planning & budgeting & project management

Level 1 Manual
• Formal systems and documented processes do not exist
• Primarily paper- or worksheet-based, with or without a CMMS
• Work relies on extensive person-to-person communications & *Heroic Efforts*

Path to Success

Figure 4 – OPM Maturity Levels Overview

Another very important perspective to highlight is that we anticipate that achieving a Level 5 state will not and should not necessarily be the strategy for every school and institution. It is very important that each organization's OPM should be synergistic with the institution's overall strategic goals and aspiration. If the senior leaders have set goals to become an industry leader with best-in-class operational processes, then we would anticipate that the organization would set its sights on achieving Level 3, then Level 4, and ultimately Level 5 performance results. On the other hand, it is understandable and acceptable that many schools and campuses do not have the resources, requirements, and expectations to become an industry leader. Achieving Level 2 results in the next 36 months may be a very practical and realistic goal for their organization.

The following diagram illustrates what we anticipate would be the prudent strategy for two hypothetical organizations, along the lines of a tactical goal of achieving the next level within one to three years. These institutions may potentially also have established a strategic goal of achieving the following performance level within the next five to ten years.

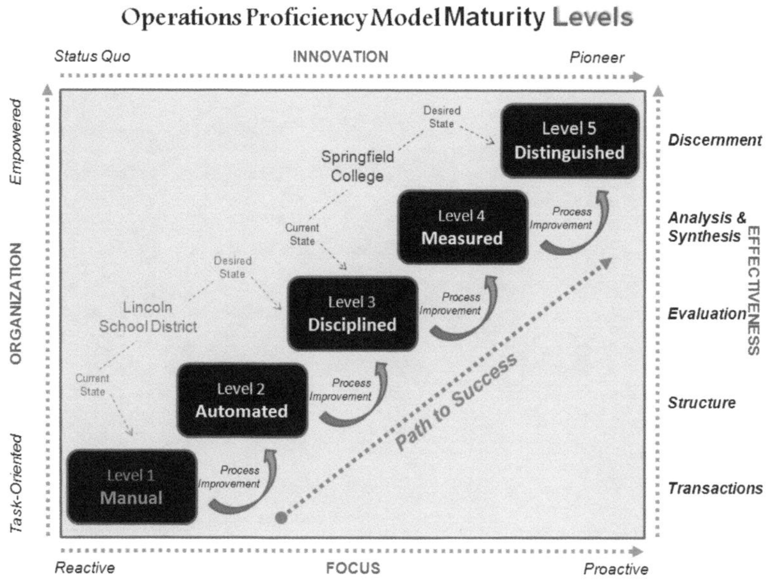

Figure 5 – OPM Tactical and Strategic Goals

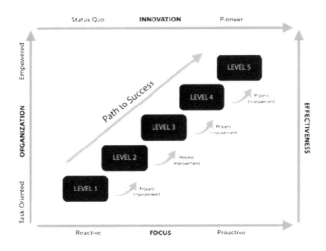

OPM Functional Disciplines

"He uses statistics as a drunken man uses lamp posts – for support rather than illumination."
– Andrew Lang

We have identified four (4) core operational **Functional Disciplines** based on our experience designing, developing, deploying, and supporting schools and higher education institutions over the past several decades. These disciplines are highlighted in the following illustration.

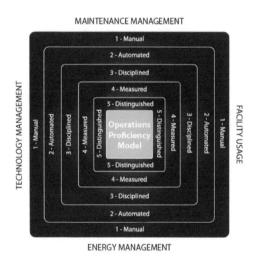

Figure 6 – OPM Functional Disciplines

The overarching disciplines from a performance management perspective include:

1. **Maintenance** Management
2. **Facility Usage**
3. **Energy** Management
4. **Technology** Management

Maintenance Management responsibilities typically include:

- Emergency Work Orders
- Corrective Work Orders
- Preventive Maintenance
- Storerooms and Inventory Management
- Custodial Services
- Grounds Management
- Fleet Maintenance
- Equipment / Asset Inventory Management
- Pest Management

Facility Usage responsibilities typically include:

- After School Event Coordination
- Event Set-up and Breakdown Scheduling
- Community Use Event Planning
- Community Use Facility Scheduling
- Community Use BAS Scheduling
- Community Use Approval Process
- Community Use Cost Recovery
- Community Use Liability and Risk Management

Energy Management responsibilities typically include:

- Normal Building Operations
- Utility Tracking and Auditing
- Utility Consumption Analysis

- Building Automation Integration
- Energy Conservation Management

Technology Management responsibilities typically include:

- Technology Services Help Desk
- Technology Services Incident Tracking
- Technology Services Problem Resolution
- Technology Asset Inventory Management
- Technology Services Hardware and Software Provisioning
- Telecommunications Equipment Provisioning
- Technology Services Hardware Life Cycle Management
- Technology Services Software Life Cycle Management
- Technology Services Applications Life Cycle Management
- Telecommunications Life Cycle Management
- Business Continuity Planning

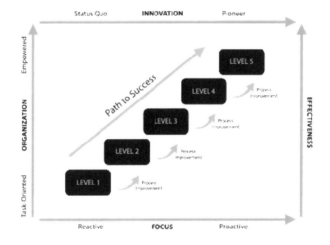

OPM Leadership Dimensions

"Management is doing things right; leadership is doing the right things."
— Peter F. Drucker

We identified a model of key **Leadership Dimensions** to support the development of *Performance Characteristics* and *Key Performance Indicators* for each operations *Discipline*. We used the following categories to describe the various capabilities and duties required to maintain and operate schools and campuses.

1. Organization
2. Process
3. Technology
4. Planning
5. Measurement

Each of the Leadership Dimensions includes ten (10) distinct Capabilities. We have included illustrations below of how these leadership elements might be defined for your institution.

Organization Leadership Dimensions

1. **Staffing** – Policies and supporting planning processes to ensure that approved positions are filled with qualified associates.
2. **Training** – The level of investment of new training and learning opportunities for existing staff.
3. **Competence Levels** – Indication of the ability of staff members to effectively and consistently perform the functions of their jobs.

4. **Recruiting and Assimilation** – Degree to which effective and efficient recruiting, on-boarding, and assimilation processes have been established and are adhered to.
5. **Goal-Setting** – Indication that organizational and individual goals are defined and monitored on a consistent basis.
6. **Performance Management** – Degree to which staff performance is evaluated versus responsibilities and goals and that appropriate feedback is provided and actions are taken as warranted.
7. **Accountability** – Degree to which staff members clearly understand role and responsibilities and are held accountable for actions and results.
8. **Empowerment** – Extent that staff members are entrusted with the support and authority to perform assigned tasks and responsibilities.
9. **Decision-Making** – Level that quality decisions are made in a structured and orderly fashion with the appropriate information that has been disseminated at the right level in the organization.
10. **Enterprise Alignment** – Degree to which goals and objectives are prioritized and aligned throughout the institution from the highest institutional level through each department, management level, and staff member.

Process Leadership Dimensions

1. **Incident Management** – Effectiveness of an organization to efficiently respond to unplanned service interruptions.
2. **Problem Management** – Effectiveness of an organization to efficiently identify the root cause of incidents and respond appropriately.

3. **Change Management** – Ability of an organization to efficiently reengineer existing processes and institutionalize new processes.
4. **Standardized Procedures** – Degree that core processes are defined and documented in the organization.
5. **Repeatable Processes** – Extent that high quality and consistent results are delivered from an organizational process.
6. **Institutionalized Processes** – Degree that core processes have been defined; documented; and staff has been trained and demonstrated proficiency to the extent that the processes are executed in a consistent manner producing consistent results.
7. **Communications** – Extent that communication occurs naturally across the organization with the right information at the right time to the right target audience.
8. **Reliability** – Degree that high quality products and services are delivered in a consistent and timely fashion.
9. **Risk Management** – Extent that management and staff members make decisions and perform assigned tasks with a high level of understanding of the potential risks and alternatives.
10. **Supplier Management** – Degree that supplier relationships are proactively prioritized and categorized with appropriate levels of accountability assigned with both organizations.

Technology Leadership Dimensions

1. **Enterprise Systems** – Extent that automated solutions are implemented and utilized to improve the productivity and effectiveness of your organization.

2. **Technology Maturity** – Degree that an organization has adopted the appropriate current best practices technologies to improve productivity and effectiveness.

3. **Business Synergy** – Extent that an organization's goals and results are aligned with the institution, and the organization is viewed as a critical and strategic element of the institution.

4. **Enterprise Integration** – Degree that core processes, systems, and data are accurate and integrated across the institution.

5. **Process Automation** – Extent that core processes have been automated and integrated across the institution.

6. **Technology Currency** – Degree that an organization has adopted the appropriate current best practices for automated solutions to improve productivity and effectiveness.

7. **Life Cycle Management** – Extent that an organization has defined and implemented processes and assigned accountability to manage the life cycle of critical systems and technologies.

8. **Enterprise-Wide Deployment** – Degree that access has been granted for key systems and data to appropriate individuals throughout the organization.

9. **Ubiquitous Access** – Ability to effectively, efficiently, and securely execute core processes regardless of physical location.

10. **Security** – Degree that security policies have been implemented and adhered to, and the extent that proactive security monitoring tools have been effectively implemented.

Planning Leadership Dimensions

1. **Resource Scheduling** – Degree that resources and equipment have been scheduled and utilized in an optimal fashion.
2. **Resource Management** – Extent that staff, equipment, tools, and supplies are defined and managed effectively and efficiently.
3. **Requirements Management** – Degree that internal and external customer requirements are understood and responded to effectively.
4. **Project Planning** – Extent that appropriate plans are developed and executed to optimize the organization's resources and assets.
5. **Project Management** – Measurement of the organization's ability to consistently develop and manage project plans effectively and efficiently.
6. **Quality Assurance** – Degree that appropriate policies and processes are in place to ensure the consistent delivery of the appropriate quality of services.
7. **Budgeting** – Extent that an efficient planning and budgeting process has been defined and implemented to produce consistent high quality financial plans for the organization.
8. **Financial Planning** – Degree that a timely and appropriate level of reviews, controls, and accountabilities are in place for financial data and results.
9. **Capital Planning** – Level of discipline, accuracy, comprehensiveness, and executive support for long-term capital funding plans to support institution.
10. **Strategic Planning** – Extent that long-term planning has been institutionalized across the organization and institution.

Measurement Leadership Dimensions

1. **Metrics-Orientation** – Extent that data is captured and used to measure and monitor core processes across the organization.
2. **Business Analytics** – Degree that business analytics tools and techniques have been deployed to support organizational and institutional process improvement.
3. **Continuous Improvement** – Extent that continuous process improvement is ingrained in the culture of the organization.
4. **Key Performance Indicators** – Degree that the organization has defined critical performance indicators and institutionalized monitoring and measuring them to support performance improvement.
5. **Peer Benchmarking** – Acknowledgment that the organization has embraced benchmarking key performance indicators with selected peers to identify best practices and performance improvement opportunities.
6. **Cross-Industry Benchmarking** – Acknowledgment that the organization has embraced benchmarking key performance indicators with leaders across multiple industries to identify best practices and performance improvement opportunities.
7. **Governance** – Degree that appropriate and effectiveness governance and controls have been institutionalized to optimize the use of financial and human resources.
8. **Customer Satisfaction** – Extent that an organization is proactively soliciting, measuring, and evaluating feedback from their internal and external customers.
9. **Strategic Goals** – Degree that relevant goals are consistently established and measured, and results are compared to goals on a timely basis.

10. **Service Level Objectives** – Extent that specific
    Service Level Objectives (SLOs) are defined,
    measured, and institutionalized across the
    organization.

We have identified these **Leadership Dimensions** to assist
towards the identification of *Performance Characteristics*
and *Key Performance Indicators*. They can also be used as
a gauge to assist you in determining your current level of
proficiency and performance; and perhaps more importantly,
your desired target level of organizational performance.

Please refer to the Appendix for an illustration of a set of
Capabilities by *Leadership Dimension* and *Proficiency
Level* that can be used as a template to generate a set of
Capabilities uniquely applicable to your organization.

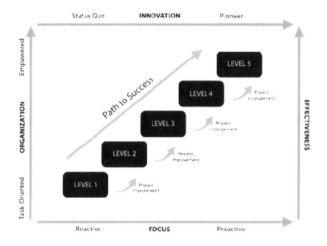

OPM Performance Characteristics

"The essence of strategy is choosing what not to do."
– Michael Porter

As described in the introduction, we recommend identifying a set of **Performance Characteristics** to be used as a guide for determining the *Level* of performance for each *Discipline* within the OPM and for identifying appropriate *Key Performance Indicators*. Our guidelines for specific Performance Characteristics for each operations Discipline are outlined below.

Please refer to the Appendix for illustrations of **Performance Characteristics** for each of the **OPM** *Disciplines* that can be used as a template to define a unique and appropriate set of characteristics specifically for your organization.

For illustrative purposes, we have included several examples of **Performance Characteristics** from each *Discipline* in our model.

Maintenance Management

Level 1 (Manual)

- Paper-Based Processes

Level 2 (Automated)

- Work Management System Utilized (i.e. CMMS)
- Roles and Responsibilities Defined
- Documented and Standardized Processes

- Basic Project Management Techniques Employed

Facility Usage

Level 3 (Disciplined)

- On-Line access for Customers to schedule events
- Defined policies on community use of facilities
- Assigned Process Owner for Facility Usage
- Published rate structure for facilities and services

Energy Management

Level 4 (Measured)

- Integration with BAS for scheduling
- Audit program to review program effectiveness
- Customer Satisfaction Surveys and Tracking
- Benchmarking against industry peers

Technology Management

Level 5 (Distinguished)

- IT Project Portfolio Management planning process
- IT Application Portfolio Management planning
- Formal enterprise architecture planning process
- Technology Department as an enterprise innovation change agent

OPM Key Performance Indicators

"In God we trust, all others bring data".
— W. Edwards Deming

Key Performance Indicators, typically referred to as KPIs, provide you with insight and perspective on your organization's performance. They become the foundation of your performance management and continuous improvements initiatives for your organization. KPIs are most effective when they are aligned with the strategic goals and objectives of your organization and the enterprise at large. Ideally, your KPIs should be relevant to your organization and aligned with the mission of your school, district, or institution.

For illustrative purposes, we have included several examples of KPIs for each operations Discipline, which are listed in the following sections.

Technology Management

Level 2 (Automated)

- Number of annual technology incidents submitted per student
- Average incident response time

Facility Usage

Level 3 (Disciplined)

- Number of community facility usage events per year per student

- Average facility usage cost recovery per event
- Average facility usage cost recovery per student
- Percentage of total community facility usage requests on-line from customers
- Percentage of facilities available versus total facilities booked

Energy Management

Level 4 (Measured)

- Percentage of total energy spend tracked monthly
- Percentage of district buildings that recycle
- Average EPA Portfolio Manager Rating
- Percentage of energy usage with real-time metering

Maintenance Management

Level 5 (Distinguished)

- Number of maintenance employees versus planners
- Percentage of stock outs
- Percentage improvement in customer satisfaction ratings
- Average asset Mean Time Between Failures (MTBF)

OPM Implementation Success Methodology

"95% of a problem is due to the process, only 5% due to the people."
– Edwards Deming

To set expectations appropriately, identifying performance characteristics and key performance indicators is quite often the easy part of implementing a performance management program. There are many additional elements that must be anticipated and addressed to ensure your performance management initiatives produce the desired results.

We have defined this effort into three key process areas that include:

1. **Translating Strategic Enterprise Goals into Departmental and Staff Goals**

2. **Establishing Accountability to Achieve Goals**

3. **Executing to Realize Goals**

Additional background information on each of these process areas is included in the following sections.

Strategy Translation Process

Figure 7 – Strategy Translation Process

Arguably the most critical element in this organizational process is ensuring that the goals and objective for your school district, university system, college campus, or state agency are **aligned** from top to bottom, i.e. from the overarching goals of the institution through the specific detailed goals of each staff member. Quite often, conflict arises, inefficiencies develop, and friction ensues when goals are not aligned from end to end. We recognize that it is sometimes difficult to envision the connection between a high-level campus, or district goal, and the goals of a craft technician – but it is critical that the goals of each of your staff members are synergistic with the goals of your organization and the hierarchy of organizations within your enterprise. It is important to make certain that specific individual goals do not inadvertently result in conflicting priorities across your school, district, or campus.

Ideally your institutional, departmental, and staff goals should also be in close *alignment* with the **Performance Characteristics** and **Key Performance Indicators** that you have defined or will be defining as you implement the **Operations Proficiency Model** for your organization. Close alignment of your KPIs through the various staff and departmental to institutional goals positions you to be successful in optimizing your resources and delivering results.

When identifying and establishing goals for your organization and staff members, we recommend that you follow the guidelines provided by experts for decades to identify **SMART goals** (Specific, Measurable, Attainable, Realistic, *and* Timely [or Time-bound])[11] [12]. Your goals should be the fuel to motivate, enlighten, energize, and guide your team. Investing the time to identify clear goals is one of the most objective tools that you can implement to measure progress and your success in delivering vital services to your internal customers.

It is amazing how much drag can be placed on the productivity of your organization when each of your team members is not working with a common set of goals, values, and priorities. On the other hand, extraordinary achievements occur as the alignment of all of your resources approaches 100%. Effective alignment is the result of lubricating your operation and removing any potential friction to optimize the productivity of your resources.

---

[11] http://rapidbi.com/history-of-smart-objectives/
[12] http://goalsetting-info.blogspot.com/2012/04/smart-goals.html

When validating the alignment of your goals and resources, it is also important to look external to your institution. Maintaining positive and proactive relationships with your key suppliers and partners can provide you with a strategic competitive advantage. Investing time proactively to communicate effectively and ensure alignment quite often can eliminate serious challenges and consequences long-term.

Accountability Process

Figure 8 – Accountability Process

We believe that all organizations should maintain an **Accountability Process** or *Employee Performance Management Process* that is conducted on a scheduled basis, at least once per year, across the enterprise. This evaluation process should include all staff members throughout the institution.

The process does not need to be tedious and should not be considered as a necessary evil. The process can, and should be, streamlined and efficient. It should emphasize providing each staff member with honest, meaningful, and actionable feedback on her performance since the previous evaluation period along with a two-way discussion on the specific goals and expectations for the current evaluation period. Ideally, each associate should have the opportunity to provide written feedback on her performance along with requirements regarding training, job experience, and strategic career expectations to position her to be successful in the future.

Preparing and delivering feedback can be rather straight-forward when specific goals and performance indicators (i.e. KPIs) have been established and institutionalized. Managers and staff tend to look forward to, versus dread, periodic performance reviews once an accountability process has been institutionalized.

The most important element in this area is clearly and formally establishing expectations with each staff member and holding her **accountable** for her actions and the results that she delivers. Organizations become very inefficient and ineffective when staff accountability is not enforced consistently. A single exception in an organization when a manager *"turns a deaf ear"* on an individual performance issue can have a tremendous negative impact on peers and colleagues and ultimately the productivity of your team.

In our view, accountability does not mean punishing a staff member when something goes wrong or when a target is missed. In many cases, process issues or conflicting priorities across your organization can hinder a staff member from reaching his goals. It is critical that managers and subordinates work together collaboratively to understand the root cause of potential issues that might inhibit staff members to deliver desired results.

Realization Process

Figure 9 – Realization Process

Most importantly, this phase is a process, not a series of occasional events when it is convenient. We believe that an organization can derive remarkably more value from embracing the process, versus focusing on the value of a particular number or result. We view the Realization Process as a continuous cycle of activities that ultimately become the engine of identifying *Continuous Process Improvement* initiatives for your organization.

Key activities within this cycle include:

- Identify specific Key Performance Indicators (**KPIs**) that can be baselined, measured, and monitored;
- Defining a repeatable and potentially automated process to **Measure** the results from your KPIs;
- Scheduling time to **Monitor** your KPIs on an consistent basis;
- **Reporting** and communicating your KPIs in a clear, concise manner in the appropriate format on a recurring, scheduled basis;
- **Analyzing** your results to determine if adjustments or other actions are required;
- Making **Decisions** based on the trends of actual results and reprioritizing your resources to implement *process improvements* to address anomalies and shortcomings;
- Refocusing and **Realigning** your specific KPIs based on the insights you have gained from your investigation, analysis, and recent decisions – and resetting your goals and respective KPIs appropriately.

This process includes the research, analysis, and identification of your baseline metrics for each KPI then establishing goals or targets for each area that is measured. You should be focusing on your customers when identifying the appropriate performance indicators for your department and each staff member. It is important that the goals continue to be aligned or realigned with your institutional and departmental goals during each cycle.

Each of these three key processes described above are *synergistic* and *integrated* and should operate in the following manner.

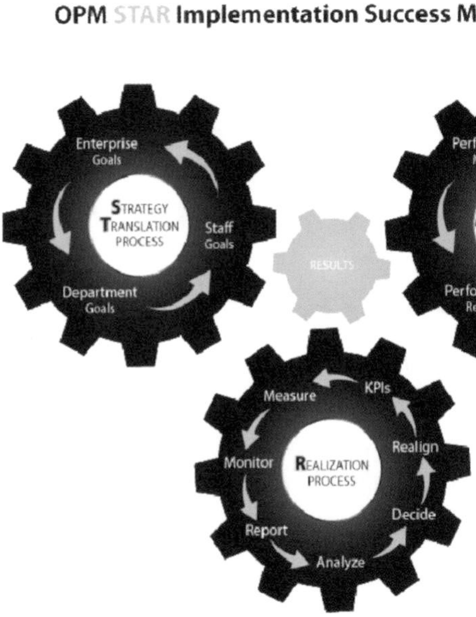

OPM STAR **Implementation Success Methodology**

Figure 10 – Organizational Performance Management Process

It is invaluable for leaders to invest time and direct resources to understand why things went wrong; did not deliver desired results; did not operate consistently; or did not produce a consistent outcome. Root Cause Analysis (RCA) techniques are a very effective method to resolve problems on a permanent basis. One technique is to use an approach referred to as "*The 5 Whys Method*" based on asking "*Why?*" five times *(from Sakichi Toyoda of Toyota Motors)* [13] to understand and uncover the "cause and effect" relationships

---

[13] http://asq.org/healthcare-use/why-quality/five-whys.html

that resulted in problems. Another effective process is to formally identify, analyze, evaluate, and document *"Lessons Learned"* based on key events that impact mission critical processes in your institution. It is important to take action on a timely basis to eliminate known problems and ultimately institutionalize any change that you have identified as a result of your analysis.

Investing time towards identifying specific metrics and performance indicators are of little value if they do not result in specific actions. It is also important to cultivate a culture that embraces identification and implementation of process improvement initiatives to continuously improve the performance of your organization.

Guidelines for Setting Goals

We offer the following guidelines for identifying goals for your organization and staff members:

1. Establish goals that are clear, concise, understandable, and presentable on a single page (when feasible) versus a long complicated document.

2. Ensure that your results are visible throughout the organization.

3. Define goals that your staff members can internalize and be held accountable for delivering results.

4. Clearly link your goals to top institutional strategies and objectives.

5. Integrate your goal-setting process with your organizational strategic planning process.

6. Develop a communications vehicle that provides a seamless, transparent drill-down capability on the details supporting your measurement processes.

7. Closely tie goals with your rewards, recognition, and compensation programs *(within the stipulations of existing contracts, policies, and regulations)*.

8. Express your specific metrics from a customer perspective.

9. Visibly demonstrate your ownership for the goals and metrics for your organization.

10. Provide the leadership to demonstrate your ability to learn from both successes and failures of your organization.

There are numerous illustrations available to assist you in developing a template for your operation. While there are numerous commercial tools available on the market today, we do not believe that you must invest in complex and expensive software to maintain a dashboard for your school, district, or campus. The key element is to update your scorecard on a scheduled basis and most importantly to use it as a tool for action in determining when course corrections are required.

The Proper Mindset for Measuring Performance

Performance Management expert, Stacey Barr, has identified *"10 Mindset Shifts to Unleash the Transformative Power of Performance Measurement"* [14] which are summarized below and synergistic with our approach for implementing performance management programs:

---

[14] http://www.staceybarr.com/howtogetkpitraining.html

1. A **continuous improvement** philosophy.
2. A **results** focus (not activity focus).
3. **Patterns**, not points (understand variation).
4. **Statistics & numbers** aren't hard.
5. Absolutely **no blame** (curiosity instead).
6. A **bias for action** (learn by doing).
7. **Process thinking.**
8. **Systems thinking.**
9. **No failure, only feedback.**
10. **Performance measurement** is PART of your job.

If implementing performance metrics is a new initiative for your organization, then you should anticipate that you will face considerable organizational *change management* hurdles and challenges. This topic is discussed in more detail in the next chapter.

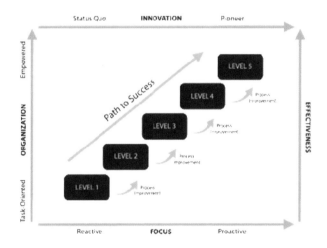

Guidelines for Effective Change Management

"There is nothing more difficult to take in hand, more perilous to conduct, or more uncertain in its success, than to take the lead in the introduction of a new order of things. For the reformer has enemies in all those who profit by the old order, and only lukewarm defenders in all those who would profit by the new order, this lukewarmness arising partly from fear of their adversaries, who have the laws in their favour; and partly from the incredulity of mankind, who do not truly believe in anything new until they have had actual experience of it. Thus it arises that on every opportunity for attacking the reformer, his opponents do so with the zeal of partisans, the others only defend him half-heartedly, so that between them he runs great danger."
— Niccolo Machiavelli, "The Prince"

It has been our observation and experience that most individuals will naturally resist being measured. Obviously there are exceptions which include athletes, sales professionals, and corporate executives. The paradox is that we need to measure performance in order to improve organizational performance. For that matter, we need to improve our performance just to maintain status quo in most environments. Bottom line is that introducing an effective performance management program, like the **Operations Proficiency Model** is not insignificant and requires *strong leadership* to achieve the maximum results. The ideal environment to successfully and efficiently implement a change initiative like **OPM** requires the commitment and alignment of leadership across the organization from top to bottom.

Managing change initiatives within any organization today is increasingly more challenging. Our internal and external customer expectations are escalating; cycle time expectations are collapsing for all business processes and transactions; geographic boundaries are collapsing as a result of globalization; organizational strategies are increasing more dynamic; every element of an organization is becoming more complex; and the traditional physical world that we know is transforming into a virtual digital workplace.

Effective change leadership is one of the most challenging and rewarding opportunities for leaders in all organizations. We believe that there are six (6) critical imperatives to prepare your organization to adapt to changing expectations.

1. Leaders must maintain a firm grasp of the **current realities**, challenges, and opportunities across the organization with proactive feedback loops and effective institutional governance.

2. Leaders must assure that the appropriate energy, enthusiasm, **priority**, and **focus** are sustained on the change initiative until the desired results have been accomplished.

3. Leaders must assemble the **right skills, talent, and attitude** on the change team to ensure that the organization will meet its overall goals for the change initiative.

4. Leaders must continuously strive to **over-communicate** the value and ultimate goals for the change initiative.

5. Leaders must be resolute and relentless towards ensuring **effective execution** of the change initiative.

6. Leaders must always strive to persevere to **institutionalize the desired change** in order to realize the goals of the change initiative.

A memorable speech, endorsement, or email from a senior executive will never be enough to drive lasting organizational change. Change initiatives require constant, consistent leadership and a commitment to produce results. As you might anticipate, performance management initiatives do require a conscious investment of key resources but offer the opportunity to deliver a tremendous **Return on Investment** of the valuable talent on your team.

As we advised earlier, it is critical to achieve full administrative leadership support *(actions and words)* for your performance management initiative. This will result in a direct correlation to your success in driving the desired change throughout your organization. It is significantly easier and faster to quell the natural resistance to these types of programs if there is unyielding support from top to bottom of your institution to achieve your goals.

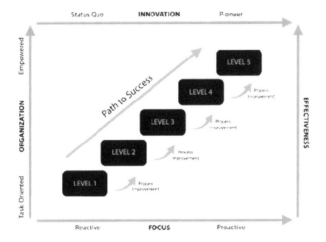

Background on the Balanced Scorecard

"The Balanced Scorecard translates an organization's mission and strategy into a comprehensive set of performance measures that provides the framework for a strategic measurement and management system."
– Robert Kaplan and David Norton, Strategy Maps

A popular and specialized manifestation of a performance management report is the **Balanced Scorecard**[15] which was developed by Robert Kaplan and David Norton in the early 1990's. Kaplan and Norton conducted extensive research on strategy-based measurement systems and identified five management principles of "strategy-focused" organizations that include:

1. Translate strategy to operational terms
2. Align the organization to the strategy
3. Make strategy everyone's everyday job
4. Make strategy a continual process
5. Mobilize change through strong, effective leadership

Their emphasis with this approach was a "balanced" measurement and monitoring process towards creating value within the enterprise. This research and findings resulted in a model that provides measurements in the following dimensions:

1. **Financial** Perspective
2. **Customer** Perspective
3. **Internal Process** Perspective
4. **Learning and Growth** Perspective

---

[15] http://www.amazon.com/Balanced-Scorecard-Translating-Strategy-Action/dp/0875846513

Key benefits from leveraging a Balanced Scorecard as a performance measurement system include:

- Providing a concise and comprehensive view on the overall health of the organization.
- Presenting a periodic glimpse into the internal operations of an organization that is traditionally difficult to obtain in most enterprises.
- Eliminating "blind spots" and sub-optimization from a singular or myopic focus on a particular opportunity within an organization.

Kaplan and Norton have also championed a concept referred to as **Strategy Maps**[16] that offers additional tools to support strategy formulation and implementation. The concept of Strategy Maps includes a taxonomy that classifies internal processes into four distinct clusters:

1. **Operations Management Processes**: Designing, producing, and delivering products and services to customers.

2. **Customer Management Processes**: Building and leveraging effective relationships with customers.

3. **Innovation Processes**: Designing and developing new products, services, processes, and enterprise relationships.

4. **Regulatory and Social Processes**: Activities to conform to regulations and societal expectations.

---

[16] http://www.amazon.com/Strategy-Maps-Converting-Intangible-Tangible/dp/1591391342/

Strategy Maps provide an organization with a logical framework for how intangible assets are linked to value-creating processes through the enterprise's strategies.

Balanced Scorecard Perspective	Operations Management Processes	Customer Management Processes	Innovation Processes	Regulatory & Social Processes
Financial Perspective				
Customer Perspective				
Internal Perspective		Map Strategic Objectives		
Learning & Growth Perspective				

Figure 11 – Strategy Maps Framework

Developing and leveraging a Balanced Scorecard is an excellent tool to attain alignment to achieve organizational goals. Successful programs require active participative engagement from all key leaders in your organization. Included below are illustrations of a Balanced Scorecard for K-12 Schools and Higher Education Institutions.

#	Perspective / Metric	Results	Goal	On Target	Trend
	Financial Perspective				
1	Maintenance & Operations Cost per Square Foot	$4.48	$4.50	☺	→
2	Maintenance & Operations Cost per Student	$911.82	$900.00	☺	↓
3	Custodial Cost per Square Foot	$1.92	$1.90	☺	→
4	Custodial Cost per Student	$327.13	$325.00	☺	→
5	Utility Cost per Square Foot	$1.38	$1.50	☺	↓
6	Utility Cost per Student	$288.46	$300.00	☺	↓
7	IT Expenditures per Student	$102.50	$125.00	☹	↓
8	Transportation Cost per Rider	$414.53	$410.00	☺	↓
9	Average Age of Fleet (Years)	16.2	15.0	☹	↓
10	Total budget expenditures within original budget	$23,850.0	$25,000.0	☺	→

Figure 12 – Public School District BSC Financial Perspective Illustration

Background on the Balanced Scorecard

#	Perspective / Metric	Results	Goal	On Target	Trend
	Customer Perspective				
1	Student Graduation Rate	88.3%	88.0%	☺	→
2	Average Daily Attendance	89.7%	90.0%	☺	→
3	Instructor overall satisfaction as measured by the Harris Poll School Pulse	8.0	8.2	☺	→
4	Staff satisfaction with condition of school buildings and grounds as measured by Harris Poll School Pulse	8.1	7.8	☺	↑
5	Parent satisfaction with condition of school buildings and grounds as measured by Harris Poll School Pulse	9.1	8.8	☺	→
6	Student satisfaction with food served in the lunchroom as measured by Harris Poll School Pulse	7.1	7.5	☹	→
7	Staff satisfaction with condition of computer technology as measured by Harris Poll School Pulse	8.4	9.0	☹	↓
9	SAT I achievement rate: Critical Reading	497	498	☺	→
10	SAT I achievement rate: Writing	487	492	☹	↓
10	SAT I achievement rate: Mathematics	516	515	☺	↑

Figure 13 – Public School District BSC Customer Perspective Illustration

#	Perspective / Metric	Results	Goal	On Target	Trend
	Process Perspective				
1	Average Work Order Completion Time (Days)	2.1	2.5	☺	→
2	Percentage of Preventive Maintenance versus Total work orders	28.0%	25.0%	☺	↑
3	Percent of major Capital Improvement Projects (CIP) completed on time and within budget	82.0%	90.0%	☹	↑
4	Percent of Help Desk Calls (tickets) resolved within 48 hours	93.4%	95.0%	☺	→
5	IT Help Desk First Call Resolution Rate	46.0%	55.0%	☹	↑
6	Ratio of Students to Computers	1.8	2.5	☺	→
7	Average Age of Computers (Years)	4.1	3.5	☹	↑
8	Percent of buses in operating condition	97.5%	96.0%	☺	↑
9	Average number of miles between per vehicle for Transportation Department Accidents	20,853.3	15,000.0	☺	↑
10	Number of Safety Incidents Recorded throughout year	3	0	☺	→

Figure 14 – Public School District BSC Process Perspective Illustration

Background on the Balanced Scorecard

#	Perspective / Metric	Results	Goal	On Target	Trend
	Innovation Perspective				
1	Percentage of teachers who are retained annually	89.9%	89.5%	☺	→
2	Percentage of staff personnel who are retained annually	79.2%	84.0%	☹	↑
3	Percentage of Buildings that Recycle	95.0%	92.0%	☺	→
4	Percentage of LEED Designed Buildings	0.0%	5.0%	☹	→
5	Percentage of Alternatively-Fueled Buses	3.0%	10.0%	☹	↑
6	Average number of hours per teacher per year for professional education	64.0	60.0	☺	↑
7	Average number of hours per staff member per year for professional education	46.0	45.0	☺	↑
8	Number of formal teacher continuous improvement initiatives approved	14	12	☺	↑
9	Number of formal staff continuous improvement initiatives approved	9	12	☹	→
10	Number of formal student continuous improvement initiatives approved	10	12	☺	↑

Figure 15 – Public School District BSC Innovation Perspective Illustration

#	Perspective / Metric	Results	Goal	On Target	Trend
	Financial Perspective				
1	Maintenance & Operations Cost per Square Foot	$4.48	$4.50	☺	→
2	Maintenance & Operations Cost per Student	$911.82	$900.00	☺	↓
3	Custodial Cost per Square Foot	$1.92	$1.90	☺	→
4	Custodial Cost per Student	$327.13	$325.00	☺	→
5	Utility Cost per Square Foot	$1.38	$1.50	☺	↓
6	Utility Cost per Student	$288.46	$300.00	☺	↓
7	IT Expenditures per Student	$102.50	$125.00	☹	↓
8	Average Age of Fleet (Years)	16.2	15.0	☹	↓
9	Budget Balance (% ot tuition & fees vs. target)	96.8%	100.0%	☹	→
10	Total budget expenditures within original budget	$23,850.0	$25,000.0	☺	→

Figure 16 – Higher Ed BSC Financial Perspective Illustration

#	Perspective / Metric	Results	Goal	On Target	Trend
	Customer Perspective				
1	Student Graduation Rate	88.3%	88.0%	☺	→
2	Student Retention Rate	89.7%	90.0%	☺	→
3	Instructor overall satisfaction as measured by the Noel-Levitz College Employee Satisfaction Survey	8.0	8.2	☺	→
4	Staff satisfaction with condition of school buildings and grounds as measured by Noel-Levitz College Employee Satisfaction Survey	8.1	7.8	☺	↑
5	Student satisfaction with academic programs (campus survey)	9.1	8.8	☺	→
6	Student satisfaction with campus services (campus survey)	7.1	7.5	☹	→
7	Student satisfaction with housing services (campus survey)	6.9	7.5	☹	↑
8	Staff satisfaction with condition of computer technology as measured by Noel-Levitz College Employee Satisfaction Survey	8.4	9.0	☹	↓
9	Student Population Diversity Score	23.0%	21.5%	☺	→
10	Student Transfer Rate	3.5%	5.0%	☺	↑

Figure 17 – Higher Ed BSC Customer Perspective Illustration

#	Perspective / Metric	Results	Goal	On Target	Trend
	Process Perspective				
1	Average Work Order Completion Time (Days)	2.1	2.5	☺	→
2	Percentage of Preventive Maintenance versus Total work orders	28.0%	25.0%	☺	↑
3	Percent of major Capital Improvement Projects (CIP) completed on time and within budget	82.0%	90.0%	☹	↑
4	Percent of Help Desk Calls (tickets) resolved within 48 hours	93.4%	95.0%	☺	→
5	IT Help Desk First Call Resolution Rate	46.0%	55.0%	☹	↑
6	Average Wireless Download Bandwidth Availability (MB)	8.0	8.2	☺	→
7	Average Age of Computers (Years)	4.1	3.5	☹	↑
8	Percent of buses in operating condition	97.5%	96.0%	☺	↑
9	Facilities Condition Index	4.3	5.0	☹	↓
10	Number of Safety Incidents Recorded throughout year	3	0	☺	→

Figure 18 – Higher Ed BSC Process Perspective Illustration

Background on the Balanced Scorecard

#	Perspective / Metric	Results	Goal	On Target	Trend
	Innovation Perspective				
1	Percentage of professors who are retained annually	89.9%	89.5%	☺	→
2	Percentage of staff personnel who are retained annually	79.2%	84.0%	☹	↑
3	Percentage of Buildings that Recycle	95.0%	92.0%	☺	→
4	Percentage of LEED Designed Buildings	0.0%	5.0%	☹	→
5	Percentage of Alternatively-Fueled Buses	3.0%	10.0%	☹	↑
6	Number of formal instructor continuous improvement initiatives approved	14	12	☺	↑
7	Number of formal staff continuous improvement initiatives approved	9	12	☹	→
8	Number of publications during school year	132.0	125.0	☺	↑
9	Number of patent applications filed during school year	8.0	12.0	☹	↑
10	Number of patents granted during school year	7	6	☺	→

Figure 19 – Higher Ed BSC Innovation Perspective Illustration

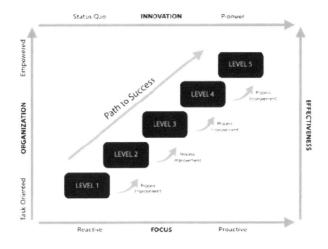

Industry Performance Benchmarking

"Benchmarking provides an inventory of creative changes that other companies have enacted."
– John Langley

Benchmarking is the process of comparing the performance of one organization against a peer or group of organizations, typically, but not exclusively within a target industry. This exercise is performed through a disciplined process of comparing a set of clearly defined and industry-accepted *Key Performance Indicators* (KPIs) across the target group. Benchmarking goals include identifying industry best practices along with specific improvement opportunities for the individual participants.

Benchmarking generally follows this sequence of events:

1. An organization or group of organizations (i.e. state association, state agency, geographical group of technical colleges, subset of large urban schools, etc.) will identify a functional area(s) that will be analyzed to compare and contrast results.

2. The initiating or sponsoring organizations will target a group of institutions to include in the benchmarking study.

3. Once the group of institutions has committed to participate in the benchmarking project; the participating schools or campuses collaborate to identify the specific performance measures that will be evaluated.

4. The next and most critical step in the process is for the participants to agree on the specific definitions and methodology of how each target performance area will be measured in order to ensure that the comparisons and results are meaningful.

5. The participants then execute their plans to capture the relevant data for the targeted performance indicators.

6. The participant data is analyzed by the review team or sponsoring organization to identify notable exceptions and anomalies and adjusted accordingly.

7. The results for all participants is consolidated to calculate statistical averages and metrics that identify top performers, means, medians and other relevant statistical measures for each metric.

8. The benchmark performance comparison reports are distributed to each participant. The benchmarking participants will decide early in the process whether specific performance results will be reported as anonymous or attributable to each participant. Quite often each participant receives a report highlighting their respective data against each participant in an anonymous fashion (i.e. District-1, District-2, District-3, etc.).

9. Each participant reviews the benchmarking reports to identify specific gaps and potential problem areas in their institution.

10. Participants prioritize the opportunities and specific initiatives that will have the most significant impact or deliver the greatest return on investment for their organization.

11. Detailed action plans for each target opportunity area are developed, prioritized, assigned target implementation or milestone dates, and resources are assigned to implement the process improvement tasks.

12. The benchmarking process is repeated periodically, typically on an annual basis. The target performance indicators are renegotiated by all participants prior to launching the next benchmarking exercise. Please note that many leading schools and campuses have already embraced continuous process improvement and have institutionalized continuous benchmarking and analysis into their culture.

While some organizations or associations will choose to initiate and manage their own benchmarking projects, many groups will choose to outsource the coordination, consolidation, and benchmark reporting to an independent external benchmarking services business. There are hundreds of businesses that offer benchmarking services and many specialize and target specific industries, like education. There are also numerous industry associations that facilitate benchmarking activities like APPA[17] and The Council of the Great City Schools[18]. SchoolDude provides benchmarking services for their clients through the SchoolDude Community[19] offering.

Included below are several illustrations of benchmarking your operational KPIs against other schools or campuses.

---

[17] http://www.appa.org/research/fpi.cfm
[18] http://www.cgcs.org/
[19] http://www.schooldude.com/

Maintenance Management

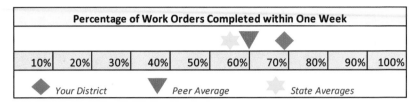

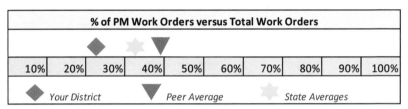

Facility Usage

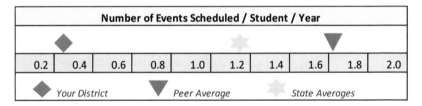

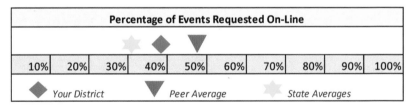

Energy Management

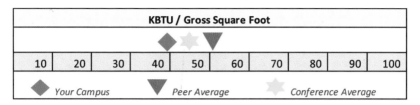

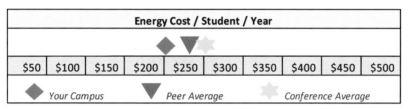

Technology Management

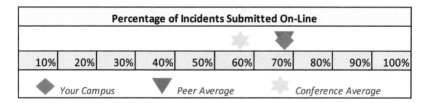

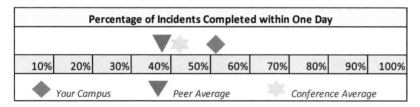

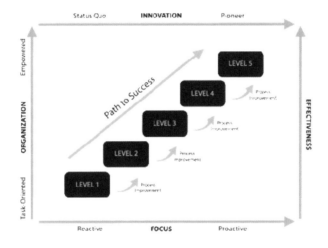

21st Century Expectations for Facilities Directors

"Effective leadership is putting first things first. Effective management is discipline, carrying it out."
— Stephen R. Covey

Doing more with less is the screenplay for Facilities Directors today – more students to serve; more square feet and acres to mow, fertilize, cultivate, clean, heat, cool, support, and maintain; and more equipment to monitor and fix. The current global economic challenges have had an impact on all industry sectors, including higher education institutions and public and private schools. Many districts and institutions have been impacted by flat or declining state budgets which have resulted in a reduction in the number of staff members to student ratio over the past several years and we suspect that this trend is not likely to reverse any time soon. On a more positive note, Facilities Directors can continue to reach out to their peers to gain insights on best practices and capitalize on new technology innovations to continue to increase productivity from year to year.

Our experience working with Facilities Directors indicates that they must be able to skillfully play the following roles:

1.   Master Craftsman

Facilities Directors first of all are required to be ambidextrous and a *"Jack of All Trades"* with a degree of competency in all disciplines of engineering including agricultural, automotive, chemical, civil, computer, electrical, electronics, energy, materials, mechanical, power, thermal, and process; as well as and finance and accounting. It is likely that many Facilities Directors confront challenges and issues in many of these disciplines on a daily basis.

2.   Thrill Seeker

Qualifications also include an innate desire to seek new adventures and challenges daily considering the millions of square feet; hundreds of acres; thousands of pieces of equipment; and thousands of students that can trigger surprises and new challenges each and every day.

3.   Champion for a Cause

In order to sustain a passion and commitment to this challenging role, Facility Directors must also maintain a fervor, fire, and zest for educating our youth and demonstrating leadership as a champion for your students, faculty, staff, parents, and the community you support. The most impactful facility leaders first and foremost have a passion for quality education at their core and set an outstanding example every day, with both words and actions, for their staff and colleagues. Passionate facilities, energy, and technology staff members and leaders are quite often revered as *"heroes"* in their buildings and campuses.

4.   Coach

Facilities Directors play a vital role as a team leader, teacher, and coach for establishing goals; identifying the specific needs and skills to support your institution; adeptly judging talent; delivering constructive feedback; and motivating your team members to achieve the right goals the right way. You need to genuinely desire that your team members succeed through leading by example; by inspiring and supporting their career aspirations; and adapting to the diverse expectations of your *Baby Boomers* through *Millennials* staff members.

5.   Tech Savvy

We continue to confront rapidly expanding technological advances from always-connected personal devices and building control systems to cloud-based application and productivity solutions. Facilities leaders need to be tech savvy to understand and embrace the technologies and resulting data resources that enable your organization to become more effective and productive each year.

6.   Multilingual

It is important that Facilities Directors be natural communicators and able to communicate with many different constituents. They must have the ability to effectively collaborate on technical issues with staff members; effectively manage expectations with faculty and staff members; review engineering specifications with architects; and discuss budgeting and capital project justifications with administration and Board members. Effective communications requires that you are proficient in speaking in a language and context that is appropriate for your target audience.

7.   Trapeze Artist

Facility Directors must also be extremely adept in prioritizing short-term tasks and long-term project initiatives with the appropriate balance of tactical challenges and strategic requirements. You must be able to change gears rapidly, smoothly transitioning between the tactical and strategic demands of your organization very responsively. It is quite likely that you will be challenged with responding to emergency break/fix requests; staff resource planning for a project; and approving a 5-year capital plan within a few hours of arriving at your office.

8.   Super Hero

Facility leaders are also expected to have the ability to look around corners, anticipating potential safety and hazard risks, and to be proactive to stop bad things from happening before they actually do. Successful Facilities Directors are proactive and are able to capitalize on their experience and instincts to foresee potential risks and avert disasters before they happen, quite often without anyone knowing about it.

9.   Strong Backbone

Facility Directors must also possess the courage and conviction to remain steadfast regarding decisions regarding safety, reliability, and quality. They must maintain currency and vigilance with applicable codes and compliance regulations. Confident facility leaders must maintain a long-term perspective with insights into how decisions impact the total cost of ownership and the overall life cycle of assets under the weight of surmounting financial, project schedule, and other tactical pressures.

10.   Institutional Leader

The most effective Facilities Directors embrace their role as a leader for their institution. They focus on aligning goals throughout the enterprise; proactively seeking peer benchmark results, best practices, lessons learned, and continuous process improvements. Their focus their natural instincts regarding when to intervene and when to empower team members. Leaders who embrace this role truly make a difference and have a considerable impact on their students and their stakeholders.

Facility Directors who are able to adeptly and continuously prioritize and focus on each of these roles will be positioned as strong and impactful leaders within your institution. They are able to optimize resources to ensure the consistent delivery of high-level quality services. The following diagram depicts the ten key roles described above.

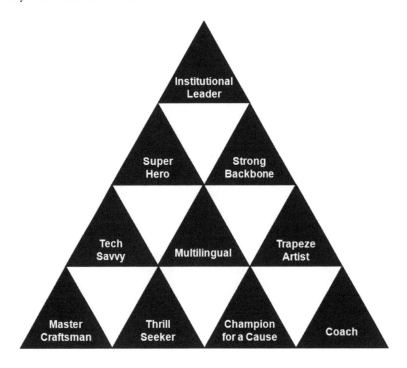

Figure 20 – 21st Century Expectations for Facilities Directors

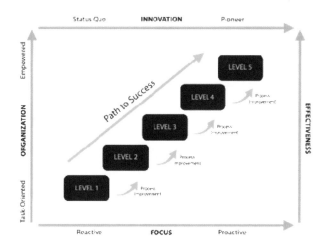

21st Century Expectations for Tech Leaders

"Management is a set of processes that can keep a complicated system of people and technology running smoothly... Leadership is a set of processes that creates organizations in the first place or adapts them to significantly changing circumstances... Successful transformation is 70 to 90 percent leadership and only 10 to 30 percent management."
— John Kotter

Rapid and potentially dramatic change is a way of life for many leaders today, and most certainly technology professionals. I have included a very small sample of the numerous factors below.

- Moore's Law (doubling of computer processor density every two years)[20]
- Collapsing technology life cycles with accelerated speeds for personal devices
- Bring Your Own Device (BYOD) management challenges
- Increasing capabilities and expectations for mobility and ubiquitous connectivity
- Increasing options for and adoption of Cloud Computing
- Emergence of analytical requirements for Big Data
- Accelerating rate of Internet connectivity for everything

Along with having to cope with increasing complexity, increasing diversity, and increasing density of technologies to

---

[20] http://www.intel.com/content/www/us/en/silicon-innovations/moores-law-technology.html

manage, technology leaders are also expected to play the following roles on a daily basis.

1.   Customer Service Agent

Leading a services-oriented and services-focused organization by action and words is a key aspect of a technology leader's job. This includes implementing Service Level Agreements (SLAs) with internal customers, suppliers, and external business partners and carefully managing expectations at all times.

2.   Ombudsman

Technology leaders must provide the leadership to proactively comply with institutional policies; local, state, and federal regulatory requirements. They are also responsible for implementing effective risk management and business continuity programs; and providing leadership to institutionalize the appropriate enterprise processes. This role also includes identifying and deploying cost effective tools for security defenses, proactive compliance monitoring, and information transparency.

3.   Drill Sergeant

Technology leaders must ensure that the right people with the right experience and the right skills can deliver an effective balance and interdependence of **Project Management, Change Management, Quality Management**, and **Financial Management** services across the institution. This requires rigorous discipline, leadership engagement, and support for key initiatives.

4.   Juggler

Technology leaders need to define and implement the appropriate level of portfolio management processes to effectively manage enterprise information technology and telecommunications investments. This includes applying industry best practices for **Application Portfolio Management** and **Project Portfolio Management** to closely align your human and financial resources with the goals and objectives of your institution.

5. Servant Leader

This role involves proactively delivering the right level of organizational leadership including optimizing your recruiting, retention, training, sourcing, performance management, compensation, and succession planning initiatives. The role of the servant leader requires you to be very attentive to what, how much, and how frequently you communicate. It also requires great judgment and intuition on when you need to be a coach and intercede in situation; and when you need to lead by empowering your team members and staying out of their way.

6. Cat Herder

Technology Directors must also have the ability to demonstrate how to develop and maintain successful partnership relationships based on appropriate prioritization of resources and identifying a win-win-win proposition *(enterprise, partner, and technology department)*.

7. Commentator

Technology leaders should develop strong skills to design and communicate the appropriate measurement processes. These core processes should be leveraged to proactively manage customer expectations and the perceptions of products and services delivered in terms that your customers can understand

and embrace. This is a combination of the "play by play" announcer and the "analyst" / "color commentator" in a sporting event.

8.   Futurist

This role includes the expectation to design and implement an effective strategic planning process that positions a technology organization to integrate and align the plans for introducing and managing technology with the long-term plans, goals, and objectives of the institution. The technology strategic planning process should be integrated with your core processes for enterprise strategic planning, enterprise architecture planning, application portfolio management, project portfolio management, and IT governance.

9.   Comptroller

Technology leaders also need to design and implement the appropriate level of technology governance-based processes. This ensures the optimal prioritization and alignment of technology-related decisions, acquisitions, and resources across the enterprise. The governance processes are integral to the core processes outlined for the "Futurist" role.

10.   Institutional Leader

Finally, all technology leaders should aspire to play a vital and strategic role in enterprise decisions that capitalize on the application of technology across the enterprise. There should be a natural evolution into this role within your district or campus as you become proficient in the other nine roles described previously.

Technology Directors who are able to adeptly and continuously prioritize and focus on each of these roles will be positioned as strong and impactful leaders within your institution. They will have achieve a level of optimized resources to ensure the consistent delivery of high-level quality services. The following diagram depicts the ten key roles described above.

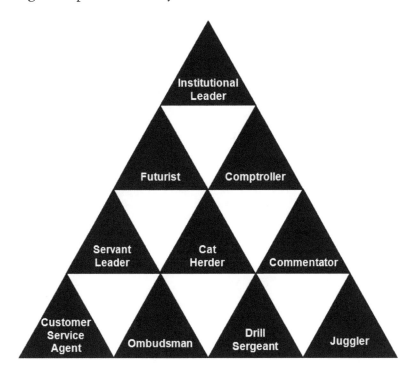

Figure 21 – 21st Century Expectations for Tech Directors

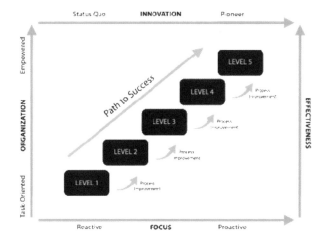

Tips for "Marketing" your Organization

*"The aim of marketing is to know and understand the customer so
well the product or service fits him and sells itself."*
— Peter F. Drucker

Marketing is an unfamiliar term to most internal operations
support organizations.

*Why should you have to think about "**marketing**" your
organization if you are not in the business of selling a product
or service to customers?*

That's a fair question, and a question that leaders should
contemplate, regardless of where you fall on an organization
chart. Let us take a closer look at what marketing really is.
According to the American Marketing Association,

*"Marketing is the activity, set of institutions, and processes for
creating, communicating, delivering, and exchanging offerings that
have value for customers, clients, partners, and society at large".[21]*

This is certainly true, but there a lot of ways to describe
marketing in the context of delivering products and services.
Included below are a few additional perspectives on
marketing from industry experts.[22]

* *"Marketing is an ongoing communications exchange with
  customers in a way that educates, informs and builds a
  relationship over time"*
* *"Marketing is meeting the needs and wants of a consumer"*

---

[21] http://www.marketingpower.com/aboutama/pages/definitionofmarketing.aspx
[22] http://heidicohen.com/marketing-definition/

- *"Marketing has little to do with the service provider and everything to do with the customer."*
- *"Marketing is delighting a consumer, customer and/or user to achieve a profit or other pre-established goal."*
- *"Marketing is a way to connect what products and services you have to offer with customers who want and need such products and services."*
- *"Marketing is anything you create or share that tells your story."*
- *"Marketing is the art and science of persuasive communication."*
- *"Marketing is the unique opportunity to establish respect and a relationship with your target audience in a way that compels them to become addicted to your products or service, your support."*

We'll start this discussion by noting that virtually all organizations have customers and suppliers, in addition to their core staff members. We find that it is a very useful perspective to view the colleagues that you support as "customers", and the individuals that provide support and services to you as "suppliers", regardless of who signs their paychecks. If you have not been proactive in describing and communicating the services that you offer, then each "customer" is left to form their own opinion based on personal experiences or hearsay, whether factual or not. We are certainly not advocating that a district maintenance office or campus technology department hire a Madison Avenue advertising agency, but we do believe that it is imperative to take a leadership role in defining the *"value proposition"* that you deliver to your internal customers.

It is important to note here that *"first impressions"* are extraordinarily challenging to change – especially overcoming negative perceptions. Do you have a realistic appreciation of the impressions that your internal customers have of your operation at various points of contact? It may be your voicemail message; work request software application; organization's website; a technician answering calls on your help desk; an office receptionist; a technician diagnosing an electrical problem in a classroom or a network connectivity issue; or a custodian cleaning the floors in the cafeteria.

Whatever that "touch point" may be, each of these interactions is either creating or reinforcing a perception of your organization. The challenge for leaders of service organizations is to understand – do each of those potential touch points represent the character of your organization that you want to portray? Is it your goal to portray your staff as professionals, experts, cost-conscious, cleanliness-conscious, health conscious, and safety-conscious – all of the above – or just the "guy" you have to deal with because you have no one else to call? Is your organization just an unavoidable cost to your district or campus, or do your internal customers appreciate the value and commitment that you deliver on a daily basis?

To further put this in context we assume that you are a member of an organization that is currently *understaffed*, *underfunded*, strapped with a substantial *deferred maintenance* or *requests backlog*, and has a long list of unfunded cost savings and cost avoidance proposals. Under these types of circumstances it may appear that marketing and communications is yet one more thing that you absolutely do not have time for. We feel quite the opposite. Strong leadership and effective communications can be a powerful weapon that results in a greater understanding and appreciation for both the challenges that you are facing and your ability to truly make a difference.

We feel strongly that data does speak volumes regarding the effectiveness of a services organization in respect to the actions, results, and deliverables from the team. When accompanied with the ability to communicate results effectively in terms that your internal customers can readily recognize and understand – it can be a remarkably powerful tool for an operations organization.

Identifying the appropriate metrics to track and communicate is the first and very important challenge. Communicating the value that your organization delivers to your internal customers is often times not a core competency of operations leaders – yet it has considerable influence on how the organization is perceived throughout the institution.

Effectively marketing the services and value that you deliver requires:

1. **The Empathy Factor.** Effectively marketing your initiatives require an investment in time to truly understand your internal customer's needs, expectations, and perspectives. We recommend taking this to the next level to gain credibility by "walking in your customer's shoes" – investing the time and effort to understand their mission, challenges, and what truly positions them to be successful.

2. **Competition for Precious Cycles.** Since most professionals today are already combating information overload, do not underestimate the value of clearly and succinctly communicating your message. Effective communication often assumes that you will have to communicate your message over and over again – using varying approaches and leveraging active listening techniques to ensure and validate that your message is understood by your stakeholders.

3. **Leverage Passion and Compassion.** Few things are more painful than having to participate in a dull, boring,

and monotonous presentation for yet one more project update or the latest coolest widget from a vendor. It makes a remarkable difference in the overall success of your meeting objectives to bring energy, passion, commitment, and determination to each opportunity you can capitalize on to share your value proposition. Use relevant and insightful stories when appropriate to sell your proposals and recommendations.

4. **Use the Language of Your Customers.** Many organizations will find it convenient to share their performance results on their website. We believe that this is an excellent idea but recommend that it will be in your best interest to display the results in a language that your internal customers and senior management can relate to and understand. Avoid the use of acronyms and highly technical terms that you and your team may be extremely comfortable with, but may likely be foreign to individuals outside of your profession. Note that many organizations find that there is tremendous benefit in investing the time to create a dashboard or scorecard to communicate your results as an alternative to publishing lists and columns of numbers.

When preparing your communications, place yourself in your target audience's "shoes", by reflecting on *(from their perspective)*:

- What's in it for me?
- How does this impact or help me?
- Is there a specific action I need to take or decision that I need to make?

An Illustration

We typically speak in terms that we are most comfortable with when presented with an opportunity to discuss your organization's contribution to your district or campus. For instance, we might share specific metrics along the lines of:

Total O&M Expenditures for District for 20xx $5,012,111
Total Energy Spend for District for 20xx $1,081,304
Number of Square Feet Maintained 1,104,888
Number of Acres Maintained 124
Total Facilities Staff Members (FTEs) June 30, 20xx 62
Number of Work Requests Received in 20xx 12,252
Number of Emergency Work Requests Received in 20xx 682
Number of Work Requests Closed within 7 days in 20xx 68.8%

These figures are important, but I suspect that many members in your Administration, School Board, or Community cannot truly relate to the magnitude of these numbers. You might want to consider normalizing your metrics on a "per student" basis along the lines of:

Average Energy Cost per Student $295.13
Average O&M Cost per Student $1,027.00
Average Capital Expenditures per Student $1.368.00
Average Cost per Public Elementary School Student for Books .. $157.21
Average Cost per Public Middle School Student for Books $225.51
Average Cost per Public High School Student for Books $255.36

As we are all familiar with, often time a picture (or chart) is a more effective means to communicate your message, along the lines of:

Tips for "Marketing" your Organization

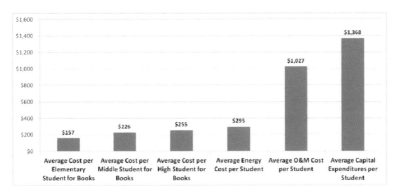

Figure 22 – Communicating Results (a)

To position your performance results even more "closer to home", you might want to reframe the conversation into a set of numbers that most of us can relate to as follows:

Equivalent # of homes supported by a school Custodial worker 14.8
Equivalent # of homes maintained by a school Maintenance worker 42.4
Equivalent # of homes maintained by a school Grounds worker 124.0
Equivalent # of Elementary School students in a home per day 17.4
Equivalent # of Middle School students in a home per day 14.5
Equivalent # of High School students in a home per day 13.3

Or, in chart form:

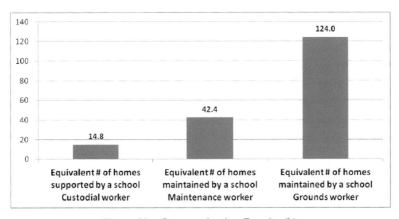

Figure 23 – Communicating Results (b)

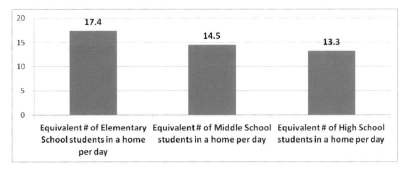

Figure 24 – Communicating Results (c)

Presenting your performance metrics in the language of your internal and/or external customers can actually produce a byproduct of "empathy" for your organization and can foster a greater appreciation for each of your staff members. Please refer to the Appendix IV for a table of national statistics that can be used as a reference to help you frame the conversation with your key external constituents.

The bottom line is that we believe it is to your advantage to be proactive in marketing your organization versus allowing your team to be taken for granted and having to reactively deal with perceptions that are not based on reality or first-hand experience. Of course there are both risks and rewards with this approach. By "putting yourself out there" versus being in "stealth mode", you may get more help from others that you have not asked for or necessarily need – i.e. other folks getting into your internal operations. On the other hand, when executed effectively, your internal marketing efforts are some of your best levers for presenting the business case to justify the resources and financial backing that you truly need.

Conclusions

"Not everything that counts can be counted; not everything that can be counted counts. Not everything that can be counted counts; and not everything that counts can be counted."
— Albert Einstein

When contemplating embracing a performance management program, like the **Operations Proficiency Model**, we believe that a successful implementation program includes three fundamental elements.

1.   Performance Management is a Process

As we stated earlier, we strongly believe that implementing an effective and successful performance management program is a ***process, not an event*** – a ***lifelong journey, not a destination***. To reap the true rewards from performance management, it is essential to cultivate a culture that embraces ***continuous process improvement***. We also strongly encourage introducing recurring ***benchmarking*** exercises into your performance management process.

2.   Strong Leadership is Essential

We suspect that many operations leaders who have already taken the steps to implement a performance management program would vouch that you will confront resistance through every step of your program. It is important to be proactive with a change management initiative to confront the challenges on a timely basis. An effective method is to capitalize on opportunities to engage team members as early in the process as possible. It is also important to invest time to educate and manage expectations with senior management early in the process.

Ultimately performance management demands timely decisions and resolute actions. The ultimate leverage you derive from your performance management initiatives is a direct result from empowering your staff to succeed simultaneously while holding them accountable to deliver results through your staff performance management program. Leaders should also proactively seek out and adopt industry best practices and encourage each member of your staff to embrace and actively participate in continuous process improvement.

3.   Proactively Managing the Change is Essential

Implementing a performance management program will require the extra emphasis, attention, leadership, perseverance, and support to successfully implement the program as an evergreen process. You should anticipate both vocal and passive resistance until you have been successful in getting all participants to understand the value that can be achieved by your organization.

Ultimately, you can achieve impressive results through the implementation of a comprehensive process that starts with setting strategic and tactical goals and expectations that drive specific actions and deliver results that are in concert with your goals. Of course, the goals of each technician all the way up the organization to your top executives must be aligned to make this possible.

As a final note, we would like to reinforce the value of using the **Operations Proficiency Model** as a tool for:

(1) **Aligning** your district or institutional **goals** with your departmental and staff objectives; along with

(2) Capitalizing on the results that your team is delivering by effectively **communicating** and **marketing** the services that your organization provides; and

(3) Leading an organization with **transparency** and **visibility** of key organization results; and

(4) Facilitating the **prioritization** of critical resources and key initiatives; and finally

(5) Using your most critical performance indicators as a catalyst for **continuous process improvement** for your organization.

We applaud your interest and desire to initiate a performance management program, and we wish you tremendous success towards achieving desired results on your *Path to Success* beyond your greatest expectations.

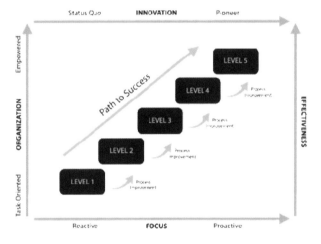

Brief History of Performance Management

"In order to succeed, your desire for success should be greater than your fear of failure."
– Bill Cosby

Included below is a brief summary that includes background information on the development of operational performance management during the past century. We view *operational performance management* as the evolution of techniques and best practices from key quality, productivity, continuous process improvement, and management systems initiatives.

The foundation of performance and quality management can be traced back hundreds of years to **Craft Guilds** through the definition of standards and inspections by skilled craftsmen to differentiate the goods they produced. In the early part of the twentieth century *Frederick W. Taylor* published his *"The Principles of Scientific Management"* where he applied **statistical theory** to improve productivity and efficiency in industrial businesses. He also introduced the concepts of **functional specialization, process analysis,** and **quality control.**

Several key quality control pioneers emerged from Western Electric beginning in the 1920s including *Walter Shewhart, George Edwards, W. Edwards Deming,* and *Joseph M. Juran.* Dr. Shewhart applied statistical approaches to the process of quality control and introduced **control charts** and a focus on eliminating variation in a manufacturing process. Shewhart also created the **Shewhart Learning and Improvement Cycle** (which Deming later popularized as the **Plan ➜ Do ➜ Check ➜ Act** cycle).

After World War II Shewhart's protégés Deming and Juran were sent to Japan under General MacArthur's Rebuilding Plan. Deming trained hundreds of Japanese managers, engineers, and academics on the benefits and value of **Statistical Process Control** (SPC). Deming later introduced elements of his quality philosophy which included his *"Seven Deadly Diseases"* of management and his *"Fourteen Points of Quality"*. His insights were eventually embraced in the US beginning in the early 1980s with corporations like Ford Motor Company and General Electric.

Joseph Juran was also a key contributor to Japan's quality movement in the 1950s and introduced the **Pareto Principle** (or 80/20 Rule) and his **Quality Trilogy** *(quality planning, quality improvement, and quality control)*. Juran's book *"Managerial Breakthrough"* is the foundation of the **Six Sigma** quality movement that became quite popular in the US beginning in the mid-1980s with corporations like Motorola and GE.

The **Toyota Production System** (TPS) introduced us to **"just in time production"**, and was the inspiration behind the **"lean"** manufacturing and "lean" techniques popular today. TPS was developed by *Taiichi Ohno, Shigeo Shingo*, and *Eiji Toyoda* beginning in the **late 1940s** through the mid-1970s. Their management philosophy emphasized business interactions with suppliers and customers along with efficiency and elimination of waste in the production and supply chain processes.

Quality Circles were introduced in Japan in the early 1960s by Kaoru Ishikawa as a means to engage the workforce to recognize, analyze, and identify solutions to work-related problems. While prevalent worldwide, this concept was not widely adopted in the US.

The **Zero Defects** quality control principles were designed as an element of Martin Marietta Corporation's Titan Missile Program in the late 1960s. These concepts were inspired by one of *Philip Crosby*'s *Four Absolutes of Quality Management*.

The concept of defining **Service Level Agreements** (SLAs) emerged as early as the 1960s in the Information Technology and Telecommunications industry as a tool to establish expectations and contracts for the delivery of technology services. SLAs continue to be an integral part of service contracts in the technology and other industries.

Reliability-Centered Maintenance (RCM) evolved from the commercial aviation industry in the 1960s as a process to establish safe minimum levels of maintenance and improve an organization's preventive and predictive maintenance programs.

Total Productive Maintenance (TPM) also originated in Japan in the early 1970s as a method for improved machine availability through better utilization of maintenance and production resources. It is based on a philosophy of understanding the elements in your job that impact the performance of key assets. TPM includes three key goals – **zero product defects; zero equipment unplanned failures;** and **zero accidents.**

Total Quality Management concepts evolved from the teachings of Deming, Crosby, Juran, and Feigenbaum. This management philosophy embraced **continuous process improvement** and was adopted by numerous businesses across multiple industry sectors over the past several decades. Another important performance concept that migrated from Japan to the US is known as **kaizen,** popularized by *Masaaki Imai,* is the management philosophy of making logical continual incremental improvements on a daily basis.

The impact of the quality movement on the electronics and automotive industry started to catch the attention of executives in the US in the 1970s.

Lean initiatives focus on improving processes with an emphasis on reducing waste, or any expenditure of resources that does not add value to your end customer. Lean Manufacturing is a direct descendent of the *Toyota Production System* (TPS). *Lean* and *Six Sigma* concepts have been merged to create **Lean Six Sigma** in the past decade. Several colleges and universities have also recently embraced **Lean Higher Education** to address the current challenges of increasing demand and decreasing supply of resources.

The concept of **Management Dashboards** became popular during the late 1970s and 1980s with the emergence of **Decision Support Systems** (DSS) and **Executive Information Systems** (EIS) as methods to use graphs, charts, images, and pictures to communicate key performance indicators and other relevant management data for the enterprise. Dashboards were conceived based on the design of a cockpit in an airplane or the dashboard in an automobile, and the concept has evolved tremendously over the past few decades with the transition from characters on a mainframe computer terminal to the highly graphical web pages that are standard today.

The *Software Engineering Institute* (SEI) at Carnegie Mellon University released their **Capability Maturity Model** (CMM) in the late 1980s. The CMM was inspired from Statistical Process Control (SPC) technically and initially designed by *Watts Humphrey* who joined the SEI in 1986 after a career with IBM. This model provided software engineering organizations with a framework to describe best practices for developing software through a series of maturity levels. Since that time, the CMM has been enhanced and expanded considerably and has been widely adopted by technology organizations.

The **Six Sigma** statistical methods were developed at *Motorola* in the mid-1980s and subsequently embraced and adopted at global corporations like GE. Six Sigma also has a foundation of continuous process improvement with a focus on removing the root causes of defects with a goal of minimizing process variability. A "six sigma process" is based on setting targets where 99.99966% of the products manufactured are free from defects, the equivalent of 3.4 defects per million. Motorola established a "six sigma" culture for all of their manufacturing operations.

The **Malcolm Baldrige** *(former US Secretary of Commerce)* **National Quality Award** was initiated by the US Congress in 1987 to recognize businesses, heath care institutions, and non-profit organizations that adopted quality management principles which have increased US competitiveness. The Baldrige Performance Excellence Program also includes **"Education Criteria for Performance Excellence"**[23] in which *"Measurement, Analysis, and Knowledge Management"* are key evaluation criteria for determining performance management. The **Baldrige Award winners in Education** are displayed on the NIST website.[24]

The *International Organization for Standardization* (ISO) published the initial version of the **ISO 9000** quality management systems standards in the late 1980s which was based on the BS 5750 series of standards from the *British Standards Institution* (BSI). The standards have been amended several times since 1987 through 2008. Currently

---

[23] http://www.nist.gov/baldrige/publications/education_criteria.cfm
[24] http://patapsco.nist.gov/Award_Recipients/AwardRecipients.cfm?sector=Education

over one million organizations globally have been independently certified as compliant with the ISO 9001 standards.

The **OGC** (British Office of Government Commerce) published a collection of service management guidelines for information technology organizations in the form of the IT Infrastructure Library (**ITIL**). ITIL is comprised of a "set of books" that includes best practices for managing IT Services around People, Processes, and Tools. The initial set of 31 books was published in the late 1980's and was focused on IT service provision. A major ITIL refresh was published as Version 2 in the late 1990's which consolidated the best practices into seven books. A third version was published in 2007, and a fourth in 2011 which consist of five core books describing the service lifecycle. ITIL has been adopted by hundreds of thousands of businesses and institutions globally as a method to create a world-class services-oriented organization.

The concept of **Business Process Reengineering** was pioneered by Professor *Michael Hammer* from MIT in **1990**[25]. Hammer suggested a rather radical approach to evaluating all of your key business processes with a goal of eliminating or restructuring any process that did not add value to your customers. The concept was aggressively embraced by many large corporations during that decade to improve their competitiveness in the global marketplace.

The **Balanced Scorecard** model for performance management reports was developed by *Robert Kaplan* and *David Norton* in the early 1990's. This model emphasized "strategy-focused" organizations and recommends a "balanced" measurement and

---

[25] http://hbr.org/1990/07/reengineering-work-dont-automate-obliterate/ar/1

monitoring approach that includes four "perspectives" to measure overall performance in an organization *(refer to the chapter on "Background on the Balanced Scorecard" for additional details)*.

The *National Association of College and University Business Officers* (NACUBO) initiated the development of the **Facility Condition Index** (FCI) in the early 1990s as a facilities management benchmarking tool that is used to compare the relative condition of a group of facilities. The FCI is calculated as a ratio of the cost of deferred maintenance to the current replacement value and is typically captured during a Facility Condition Assessment of an enterprise.

The *APQC* (American Productivity & Quality Center) developed the **Process Classification Framework** (PCF) in the early 1990s as a high-level, industry-neutral enterprise model and taxonomy that allows organizations to benchmark their activities from a cross-industry process viewpoint. The most recent version of the **APQC Process Classification Framework (PCF) for Education** was released in early 2013.

The process of comparing your performance results with another organization and/or industry best practices, referred to as **Benchmarking**, became very popular amongst information technology organizations beginning in the 1990s. There are numerous industry organizations and professional consulting businesses that support and facilitate the benchmarking process in most industries today.

An initiative by the *Project Management Institute* (PMI) to document industry standard project management best practices was published as a formalized "Guide to the Project Management Body of Knowledge" (**PMBOK Guide**) in the mid 1990s. The PMI also initiated a certification process for professional project managers who can be accredited as a Project Management Professional (**PMP**) through a series of coursework and examinations.

The *ISACA* *(formerly known as the Information Systems Audit and Control Association)* introduced a framework in the mid-1990s for effectively managing and governing information technology initiatives referred to as the Control Objectives for Information and Related Technology (**COBIT**). The latest version, COBIT 5 was released in mid-2012 and includes five key principles for the governance and management of enterprise information technology resources.

Triple Bottom Line (TBL or 3BL) is a framework for establishing goals in the context of three pillars, "People", "Planet", and "Profit". The phrase was initially coined by *John Elkington* and published in *"Cannibals with Forks: the Triple Bottom Line of 21st Century Business"* in 1997.

In the early 2000s the *TM Forum* (TeleManagement) published **eTOM** *(enhanced Telecom Operations Map)* business process framework as a guidebook of best practices for the Telecommunications industry.

The Association of School Business Officials International *(ASBO)* with support from the National Center for Education Statistics *(NCES)* and School Facilities Maintenance Task force published the **"Planning Guide for Maintaining School Facilities"** in 2003 which included checkpoints for key maintenance areas.

APPA *(formerly known as the Association of Physical Plant Administrators)* released their current generation of the **Facilities Performance Indicators** (FPI) report for each school year beginning with 2003-2004. The reports provide a representative set of statistics about facilities in educational institutions. This survey and benchmarking service is being utilized by hundreds of institutions across North America and includes aggregated data on costs and assets for the survey participants.

The Office of Government Commerce *(OGC)* in the UK created the **P3M3** (Portfolio, Program, and Project Management Maturity Model) in 2006 as a reference guide which includes best practices and **Key Process Areas** (KPAs). It was based on the process maturity framework from the SEI Capability Maturity Model described above and is used to manage technology resources and initiatives.

The *Council of Great City Schools* launched their **"Managing for Results in America's Great City Schools: A Report of the Performance Measurement Benchmarking Project"** initiative in 2007 with *ActPoint* [26] to identify key performance indicators for large school districts in the areas of transportation, food services, maintenance and operations, procurement, and safety and security. The benchmarking report initially included 50 indicators, and now incorporates over 300 Key Performance Indicators (KPIs).

The *Department of Housing and Public Works in Queensland*, Australia recently published their **Maintenance Management Framework** (MMF) and **Building Asset Performance Frameworks** (BAPF) to facilitate effective decision-making in regard to building management.

---

[26] http://www.actpoint.com/

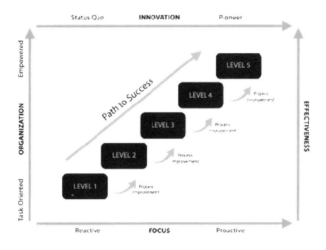

Appendix I: OPM Leadership Dimensions Illustrations

Included below are illustrations of how an organization might develop a set of key **Leadership Dimensions** to support the development of *Performance Characteristics* and *Key Performance Indicators*. OPM templates are available at http://www.schooldude.com/opm.

Organization Leadership Dimensions

Dimensions | Capabilities	Level 1 Manual	Level 2 Automated	Level 3 Disciplined
1 Staffing	Reactive	As Time Permits	Proactive
2 Training	On the Job Training	As Required	Just-in-Time
3 Competence Levels	Fire Fighting	Heroes	Competent Staff
4 Recruiting & Assimilation	As Needed	Limited Process	Structured Processes
5 Goal-Setting	Reactive	Tactical	Annual Goal-Setting
6 Performance Management	Reactive	Informal	Formal
7 Accountability	Organization Only	Selective	Documented
8 Empowerment	Command & Control	Hierarchical	Selected
9 Decision-Making	Reactive	Tactical	Defined
10 Enterprise Alignment	Organizational Islands	Department Aligned	Some Cross-Organizational

Dimensions | Capabilities	Level 4 Measured	Level 5 Distinguished
1 Staffing	Formalized	Succession Plans
2 Training	Planned	Continuous
3 Competence Levels	Competent Staff	Highly Competent Staff
4 Recruiting & Assimilation	Comprehensive	Highly Efficient
5 Goal-Setting	Quarterly Reviews	Continuous
6 Performance Management	Strategic	Strategic
7 Accountability	Embraced	Institutionalized
8 Empowerment	Decision-Makers	Enterprise-wide
9 Decision-Making	Efficient	Highly Efficient
10 Enterprise Alignment	Goal-Driven	Highly Synergistic

Process Leadership Dimensions

Dimensions | Capabilities	Level 1 Manual	Level 2 Automated	Level 3 Disciplined
1 Incident Management	Reactive	Incidents Captured	Process Defined
2 Problem Management	Reactive	Problems Captured	Process Defined
3 Change Management	Reactive	Some Planning Introduced	Process Defined
4 Standardized Procedures	Ad Hoc	Critical Procedures Introduced	Procedures Defined
5 Repeatable Processes	Ad Hoc	Critical Processes Introduced	Accountabilities Defined
6 Institutionalized Processes	Ad Hoc	Processes Introduced	Repeatable Processes
7 Communications	Event Driven	As Required	Proactive Communications
8 Reliability	Ad Hoc	Reliability Introduced	Consistent Deliverables
9 Risk Management	Ad Hoc	High Level Understanding	Analysis of Risks
10 Supplier Management	Event Driven	As Required	Responsibilities Defined

Dimensions | Capabilities	Level 4 Measured	Level 5 Distinguished
1 Incident Management	Incidents Measured	Institutionalized
2 Problem Management	Problems Measured	Institutionalized
3 Change Management	Change Management Planning	Institutionalized
4 Standardized Procedures	Structured Library	Institutionalized
5 Repeatable Processes	Consistent Delivery	Institutionalized
6 Institutionalized Processes	Processes Measured	Institutionalized
7 Communications	Formal Communication Processes	Institutionalized
8 Reliability	Reliability Measured	Institutionalized
9 Risk Management	Formal ROI & Risk Analysis	Institutionalized
10 Supplier Management	Relationships Measured	Institutionalized

Technology Leadership Dimensions

Dimensions | Capabilities	Level 1 Manual	Level 2 Automated	Level 3 Disciplined
1 Enterprise Systems	Limited, Non-Existent	Automated Business System	Integrated Business Systems
2 Technology Maturity	PC-based	Multi-User Systems	SaaS [Cloud-based] Solutions
3 Business Synergy	Independent Org Unit	Goals in Concert with Enterprise	Synergy with Enterprise Goals
4 Enterprise Integration	Paper-based Integration	Independent Business Systems	Multiple Integration Points
5 Process Automation	Primarily Manual Processes	Initial Process Automation	Inter-functional Processes
6 Technology Currency	Unsupported Legacy Apps	Vendor Supported Applications	SaaS-based Solutions
7 Life Cycle Management	Tactical, As Prompted	Annual Review Process	Product Manager Assigned
8 Enterprise-wide Deployment	Centralized	Limited External Access	Enterprise-wide Access
9 Ubiquitous Access	Single Point of Access	Limited Distributed Access	Mobile Access, Tablets
10 Security	Single Point of Access	Single Point Secure Access	Security Policies

Dimensions | Capabilities	Level 4 Measured	Level 5 Distinguished
1 Enterprise Systems	EAM / ERP Solutions	EAM / ERP Solutions
2 Technology Maturity	SaaS-based Enterprise Systems	SaaS-based Enterprise Systems
3 Business Synergy	Goals Synergistic w/Enterprise	Engaged in Strategic Planning
4 Enterprise Integration	Primary Integration Touchpoints	Comprehensive Integration
5 Process Automation	Integrated Enterprise Systems	Integrated Enterprise Systems
6 Technology Currency	SaaS and Mobile Solutions	Integrated Cloud Solutions
7 Life Cycle Management	Strategic Investment Reviews	Strategic Life Cycle Mgmt
8 Enterprise-wide Deployment	Proactive Enterprise Access	Secure Partner Access
9 Ubiquitous Access	Smart Phones	Secure, Ubiquitous Access
10 Security	Proactive Security Monitoring	Multiple Authentication

Planning Leadership Dimensions

Dimensions | Capabilities	Level 1 Manual	Level 2 Automated	Level 3 Disciplined
1 Resource Scheduling	Ad Hoc	Schedules Defined	Formal Scheduling Introduced
2 Resource Management	Ad Hoc	Resources Defined	Formal Resource Management
3 Requirements Management	Ad Hoc	As Required	Formal Requirements Mgmt
4 Project Planning	Ad Hoc	As Required	Formal Project Planning
5 Project Management	Ad Hoc	Worksheet-based	Project Management Introduced
6 Quality Assurance	Ad Hoc	As Required	Formal QA Introduced
7 Budgeting	As Required	Annual Budgeting Process	Annual Budgeting Process
8 Financial Planning	Ad Hoc	Financial Planning Introduced	Financial Planning Accountability
9 Capital Planning	Ad Hoc	Initial Capital Planning	Capital Planning Accountability
10 Strategic Planning	Ad Hoc	As Required	Strategic Planning Introduced

Appendix I: OPM Leadership Dimensions Illustrations

Dimensions | Capabilities	Level 4 Measured	Level 5 Distinguished
1 Resource Scheduling	Scheduling Optimized	Integrated Resource Scheduling
2 Resource Management	Resource Mgmt Optimization	Integrated Resource Management
3 Requirements Management	Requirements Mgmt Optimization	Integrated Resource Mgmt
4 Project Planning	Project Planning Measured	Integrated Project Planning
5 Project Management	Project Mgmt Measured	Staff with PMI Certifications
6 Quality Assurance	Six Sigma or Related QA Mgmt	Subscribe to ISO 9001: 2008 Std
7 Budgeting	Comprehensive Budgeting	Integrated Budgeting
8 Financial Planning	Proactive Financial Planning	Integrated Financial Planning
9 Capital Planning	Proactive Capital Planning	Integrated Capital Planning
10 Strategic Planning	Proactive Strategic Planning	Strategic Planning Institutionalized

Measurement Leadership Dimensions

Dimensions | Capabilities	Level 1 Manual	Level 2 Automated	Level 3 Disciplined
1 Metrics-Orientation	*Not Applicable*	*Not Applicable*	*Not Applicable*
2 Business Analytics	*Not Applicable*	*Not Applicable*	*Not Applicable*
3 Continuous Improvement	*Not Applicable*	*Not Applicable*	*Not Applicable*
4 Key Performance Indicators	*Not Applicable*	*Not Applicable*	*Not Applicable*
5 Peer Benchmarking	*Not Applicable*	*Not Applicable*	*Not Applicable*
6 Cross-industry Benchmarking	*Not Applicable*	*Not Applicable*	*Not Applicable*
7 Governance	*Not Applicable*	*Not Applicable*	Governance Introduced
8 Customer Satisfaction	Associate Driven	Associate Driven	Organizational SLA Goals
9 Strategic Goals	*Not Applicable*	*Not Applicable*	Strategic Goals Introduced
10 Service Level Objectives	*Not Applicable*	*Not Applicable*	SLO Defined

Dimensions | Capabilities	Level 4 Measured	Level 5 Distinguished
1 Metrics-Orientation	Metrics for Key Processes	Metrics Institutionalized
2 Business Analytics	Business Analytics Introduced	Sophisticated Business Analytics
3 Continuous Improvement	Not Applicable	CI Methodologies Implemented
4 Key Performance Indicators	KPIs Introduced	KPIs Institutionalized
5 Peer Benchmarking	Peer Benchmarking	Peer Benchmarking
6 Cross-industry Benchmarking	Not Applicable	Cross-Industry Benchmarking
7 Governance	Critical Process Governance	Optimized Governance
8 Customer Satisfaction	Organizational Surveys & Metrics	Integrated Customer Satisfaction
9 Strategic Goals	Critical Strategic Goals	Strategic Planning Institutionalized
10 Service Level Objectives	SLO Measured	SLO Institutionalized

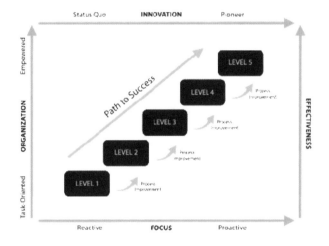

Appendix II: OPM Performance Characteristics Examples

Included below are examples of **Performance Characteristics** for each of the **OPM Disciplines** that can be used as a template to define an appropriate set of disciplines for your organization. **OPM** templates are available at http://www.schooldude.com/opm.

Maintenance Management

Level 1 (Manual)

- Paper-based Processes
- Person-to person communications

Level 2 (Automated)

- Work Management System Utilized (CMMS)
- Roles and Responsibilities Defined
- Financial Planning and Budgeting
- Documented and Standardized Processes
- Basic project management techniques

Level 3 (Disciplined)

- Customer Access to Work Order Requests
- Preventive Maintenance Program
- Inventory / Stores Management
- Planning and Scheduling Processes
- Labor and Materials Allocations
- Understanding of trends versus stated goals
- Ubiquitous (mobile) Technology Deployment
- Building Automation Systems (BAS) Integration

- Integrated Pest Management (IPM) Program

Level 4 (Measured)

- Key Performance Indicators (KPIs)
- Dashboard or Scorecard
- Capital Planning
- Sophisticated project management techniques
- Equipment Life Cycle Costing
- Partnership Management Programs
- Root Cause Analysis (RCA) Techniques
- Pareto Analysis Techniques
- Customer Satisfaction Surveys and Tracking
- Proactive Facilities Leadership
- Proactive Marketing Program
- Industry Benchmarking
- Staff Empowerment

Level 5 (Distinguished)

- Data-enriched Work Orders
- Predictive (Condition-based and/or TPM)
- Lean Maintenance Program
- Continuous Improvement Programs
- Effective Change Management Techniques
- Executive Dashboards

Facility Usage

Level 1 (Manual)

- Paper-based processes
- Person-to person communications

Level 2 (Automated)

- Roles and Responsibilities Defined
- Financial planning and forecasting
- Defined event scheduling processes
- Basic project management techniques
- Define rate structure for facilities and services

Level 3 (Disciplined)

- Customer on-line access to schedule events
- Defined policies on community use of facilities
- Assign Process Owner for Facility Usage
- Publish rate structure for facilities and services
- Understanding of trends versus stated goals
- Documented process for community use

Level 4 (Measured)

- Interactive Web-based calendar for community access
- Proactive communications program
- Integration with BAS for scheduling services
- Ability to price energy usage for events
- Automated Invoicing and Receivables process
- Automated scheduling for set-up and tear-down
- Key Performance Indicators (KPIs) defined
- Dashboard or Scorecard implemented
- Audit program to review program effectiveness
- Customer Satisfaction Surveys and Tracking
- Customer relationship management programs
- Benchmarking against Peers

Level 5 (Distinguished)

- Continuous Improvement Program Implemented
- Mobile access to facilities use calendar

Energy Management

Level 1 (Manual)

- Paper-based Processes
- Person-to person communications

Level 2 (Automated)

- Roles and Responsibilities Defined
- Financial planning and forecasting
- Event scheduling processes defined
- Basic project management techniques

Level 3 (Disciplined)

- Understanding of trends versus stated goals

Level 4 (Measured)

- Integration with BAS for scheduling services
- Key Performance Indicators (KPIs) defined
- Dashboard or Scorecard implemented
- Training and Education programs for faculty and staff
- Training and Education programs for students
- Automated classroom temperature monitoring
- Monitoring and control of relative humidity
- Audit program to review program effectiveness
- Customer Satisfaction Surveys and Tracking
- Customer relationship management programs
- Benchmarking against Peers

Level 5 (Distinguished)

- Continuous Improvement Program Implemented

- Mobile access to facilities use calendar

Technology Management

Level 1 (Manual)

- Paper-based Processes
- Person-to person communications
- Reactive incident and problem management

Level 2 (Automated)

- Automated Incident tracking
- Documented and Standardized Processes
- Roles and Responsibilities Defined

Level 3 (Disciplined)

- Service Desk processes and staffing
- IT Services Catalog defined
- IT Asset tracking
- Problem Management procedures
- Service Levels defined
- Service Request Fulfillment processes
- Project Management methodology
- Disaster Recovery procedures
- Change Management Procedures defined
- Security Management procedures
- Access Management procedures
- Customer Access to Incident Requests
- Proactive customer surveys

Level 4 (Measured)

- Customer Self-Service tools

- Configuration Management Database
- Release Management Procedures
- Service Availability tracking and analysis
- Capacity Management planning
- Service Continuity Management processes
- Total Cost of Ownership Analysis
- Financial Management planning
- Change Advisory Board
- Enterprise risk and resilience assessments
- Business Continuity Planning Process
- IT Key Performance Indicators (KPIs)
- Proactive IT Services marketing program
- Peer Benchmarking

Level 5 (Distinguished)

- IT Project Portfolio Management
- IT Application Portfolio Management
- IT Infrastructure Portfolio Management
- Formal recurring Business Continuity Drills
- Proactive Supplier Management
- Formal enterprise architecture planning
- Technology Department as a strategic business partner
- Technology Department as an enterprise innovation change agent
- Industry Benchmarking

Appendix III: OPM KPI Examples

Included below are examples of **Key Performance Indicators** for each of the **OPM Disciplines** from our database of over one thousand KPIs that can be used as a template to define an appropriate set of disciplines for your organization. **OPM** templates are available at http://www.schooldude.com/opm.

Maintenance Management

Level 2 (Automated)

- # of Work Orders per square foot of conditioned space
- # of Work Orders per student per year
- % of overall budget allocated to M&O
- % of the total work orders that include hours billed
- % of total work order requests submitted directly by customers

Level 3 (Disciplined)

- % of emergency work orders
- % of preventive work orders
- % of corrective work orders
- Maintenance Cost per Square Foot
- Maintenance Cost per Student
- Maintenance efficiency %
- % of equipment coverage by CMMS
- % of maintenance labor recorded in CMMS
- % of contract labor recorded in CMMS
- % of materials costs recorded in CMMS

Level 4 (Measured)

- Average backlog hours per maintenance staff
- Average time expended per work order
- Average closure rate for non-PM work orders
- Average closure rate for PM work orders
- # of corrective work orders completed in 24 hours
- # of corrective work orders completed in 48 hours
- # of corrective work orders completed in 72 hours
- # of corrective work orders completed in 7 days
- # of work orders submitted per FTE per year
- % of overtime versus scheduled hours
- % of contractor costs versus labor costs
- % of PM work orders completed within 28 days of schedule
- % of PM tasks completed versus scheduled
- % of PM hours completed versus scheduled
- % of Work Orders closed per technician per day
- # Emergency Job Hours / Total Hours Worked
- Deferred Maintenance amount per square foot
- Deferred Maintenance amount per student
- Number of safety incidents per maintenance staff per year

Level 5 (Distinguished)

- Maintenance inventory turns
- Total inventory value divided by the total $ of students
- # of maintenance employees versus planners
- # of rush purchase orders versus total purchase orders
- # inactive stock items versus total stock items
- % of stock outs
- Average rework hours per maintenance staff
- % improvement in customer satisfaction ratings
- Average asset mean time before failure (MTBF)
- Average cycle time between unscheduled outages

- Total asset down time caused by breakdowns

Facility Usage

Level 2 (Automated)

- % of total locations / areas / rooms defined in facilities database

Level 3 (Disciplined)

- # of community facility use events per year per student
- # of community facility use events invoiced per year per student
- Average Facility Cost Recovery per event
- Average Facility Cost Recovery per square foot
- Average Facility Cost Recovery per student
- Number of Facility Scheduling-related Work Orders generated
- % of total community facility use requests on-line from customers

Level 4 (Measured)

- Average cycle time (# of days) between requests and approval
- Total $ received divided by the total $ invoiced per year

Energy Management

Level 2 (Automated)

- % of Buildings with Gross Square Footage captured in facility system
- % of recycled versus non-recycled content procured

Level 3 (Disciplined)

- % change in total costs of all utilities per year over past 3 years
- Annual energy (utility) cost per square foot
- Annual energy (utility) cost per student
- Water Usage per Square Foot
- Energy consumption intensity (thousand BTUs per square foot)
- Energy consumption intensity (thousand BTUs per student)
- Annual energy cost per student
- Annual Energy Cost Index (ECI): Annual energy spend / total square feet
- Energy Use Index (EUI): Annual kBTUs / total square feet
- Average vehicle fuel costs per vehicle
- Total vehicle fuel costs per student
- Total vehicle fuel costs per year

Level 4 (Measured)

- % of total energy spend tracked monthly
- % of District Buildings That Recycle
- Average EPA Portfolio Manager Rating
- % of energy usage with real-time metering
- Average Degree Days by month
- % of faculty and staff trained on conservation techniques
- % of students trained on conservation techniques

Level 5 (Distinguished)

- % of buildings assigned Energy Star ratings
- % of LEED Designed Buildings
- Total CO2 Emissions from Energy Consumption

- Total CO_2 Emissions from transport to and from school per year
- Total CO_2 Emissions from Waste

Technology Management

Level 2 (Automated)

- # of annual technology Incidents submitted per student
- Average incident response time

Level 3 (Disciplined)

- % of incidents resolved during first contact
- Average problem response time
- % of service requests escalated to 2nd level support
- % of service requests reopened
- # of incidents per Known Problem
- % of changes that result in unplanned incidents
- # of security incidents causing service interruption or reduced availability
- # of monitored Service Level Agreements
- % of projects completed on schedule
- % of projects completed within project budget
- # of Shortcomings identified during Disaster Recovery Drills
- # of IT Incidents and Requests submitted by Customers on-line

Level 4 (Measured)

- # of Service Interruptions
- # of incidents due to insufficient service or resource capacity
- % of software installations resulting in unplanned incidents

- % of software upgrades resulting in unplanned incidents
- # of deviations between configuration database and actual configurations
- Actual annual results vs. budgeted costs

Level 5 (Distinguished)

- Customer Satisfaction Survey ratings per service
- # of planned actual exercises of Business Continuity Plan
- # of Business Continuity Plan training sessions conducted
- % of Contracts with Contract Managers assigned
- # of Architecture Guiding Principles defined

Appendix IV: Educational Statistics

We have included this table of educational figures to assist leaders in creating stories that tell how their operation is impacting the educational process, improving student achievement, and maximizing the return on investment from tax and/or tuition funding for the institution.

Figure	Metric	Footnote
32,100	National median square feet maintained per full-time Custodial worker	27
92,074	National median square maintained per full-time Maintenance worker	19
31	National median acres maintained per full-time Grounds worker	19
46	Average full-time Custodial workers per School District	19
12	Average full-time Maintenance workers per School District	19
4	Average full-time Grounds workers per School District	19
$295.13	Average Energy / Utilities Cost per Student (K-12)	19
$1,027.00	Average Operations & Maintenance Cost per Student (K-12)	19
$1,368.00	Average Capital Expenditures per Student (K-12)	19
600	Average number of students per Elementary School Building	19
936	Average number of students per Middle School Building	19
1,600	Average number of students per High School Building	19
75,000	Average size of a new Elementary School Building	19
140,000	Average size of a new Middle School Building	19
260,000	Average size of a new High School Building	19
125	Average square footage per Elementary School Student	Calc

---

[27] American School and University magazine 38th Annual M&O Cost Study, 2009, http://asumag.com/maintenance/38th-annual-maintenance-operations-cost-study-schools

Figure	Metric	Footnote
150	Average square footage per Middle School Student	Calc
163	Average square footage per High School Student	Calc
98,817	Number of operating public elementary / secondary schools in the US	28
33,366	Number of operating private elementary / secondary schools in the US	20
1,800,000	Charter schools enrollment	20
2,100,000	Magnet schools enrollment	20
42	Average public school building age	29
49,400,000	Number of students attending public Elementary / Secondary schools in US	30
5,800,000	Number of students attending private Elementary / Secondary schools in US	22
3,300,000	Number of teachers supporting public Elementary / Secondary schools in the US	22
500,000	Number of teachers supporting private Elementary / Secondary schools in the US	22
19,100,000	Number of students attending 2-year and 4-year colleges and universities	22
1,800,000	Number of staff and faculty working in public degree-granting institutions	22
950,000	Number of staff and faculty working in private degree-granting institutions	22
2,169	Median square footage of new single-family houses in the US	31
0.25	Median lot size for a single-family home in the US	32
125.0	Average square footage per Elementary Student	19
149.6	Average square footage per Middle School Student	19
162.5	Average square footage per High School Student	19
$157.21	Average cost per public Elementary School student for books	33

[28] http://nces.ed.gov/pubs2012/2012325.pdf
[29] http://nces.ed.gov/pubs2000/2000032.pdf
[30] http://nces.ed.gov
[31] http://www.census.gov/const/C25Ann/sftotalmedavgsqft.pdf
[32] https://www.census.gov/hhes/www/housing/housing_patterns/pdf/Housing%20by%20Year%20Built.pdf
[33] http://www.ncpublicschools.org/docs/fbs/resources/data/factsfigures/2010-11figures.pdf

Appendix IV: Educational Statistics

Figure	Metric	Footnote
$225.51	Average cost per public Middle School Student for books	25
$255.36	Average cost per public High School Student for books	25
$2,200.00	Average Annual Energy Bill for a typical Single Family home in the US	34
2.58	Average Members per Household in the US	35
14.8	Equivalent number of homes supported by a school Custodial worker	Calc
42.4	Equivalent number of homes maintained by a school Maintenance worker	Calc
124.0	Equivalent number of homes maintained by a school Grounds worker	Calc
17.4	Equivalent number of Elementary School Students in a home per day	Calc
14.5	Equivalent number of Middle School Students in a home per day	Calc
13.3	Equivalent number of High School Students in a home per day	Calc
$295.13	Average energy cost per student in US	Calc
$852.71	Average energy cost per household member in US	Calc
125	Median square footage per student in US	36
$2.36	Average energy cost per square foot for Elementary School	Calc
$1.97	Average energy cost per square foot for Middle School	Calc
$1.82	Average energy cost per square foot for High School	Calc
$1.01	Average energy cost per square foot for households in US	Calc
$179,023,756,000	Total Services Expenditures for Public Schools in US	37
$28,586,926,000	Total Pupil Support Services Expenditures for Public Schools in US	29
$24,773,416,000	Total Instructional Staff Support Services Expenditures for Public Schools in US	29

[34] http://www.energystar.gov/index.cfm?c=products.pr_pie
[35] http://www.census.gov/prod/cen2010/briefs/c2010br-14.pdf
[36] http://www.peterli.com/spm/pdfs/SchoolConstructionReport2011.pdf
[37] http://www2.census.gov/govs/school/10f33pub.pdf

Figure	Metric	Footnote
$9,591,356,000	Total General Administration Expenditures for Public Schools in US	29
$27,761,673,000	Total School Administration Expenditures for Public Schools in US	29
$48,678,859,000	Total Operation and Maintenance of Plant Expenditures for Public Schools in US	29
$22,131,859,000	Total Pupil Transportation Expenditures for Public Schools in US	29
$17,499,667,000	Total Other and Non-specific Support Services Expenditures for Public Schools in US	29
$10,615	Total Per Pupil Expenditures for Public Schools in US: Total	29
$6,468	Total Per Pupil Expenditures for Public Schools in US: Salaries and Wages	29
$2,270	Total Per Pupil Expenditures for Public Schools in US: Employee Benefits	29
$6,478	Total Per Pupil Expenditures for Public Schools in US: Instruction - Total	29
$4,376	Total Per Pupil Expenditures for Public Schools in US: Instruction - Salaries and Wages	29
$1,514	Total Per Pupil Expenditures for Public Schools in US: Instruction - Benefits	29
$3,711	Total Per Pupil Expenditures for Public Schools in US: Support Services - Total	29
$593	Total Per Pupil Expenditures for Public Schools in US: Support Services - Pupil Support	29
$514	Total Per Pupil Expenditures for Public Schools in US: Support Services - Staff Support	29
$199	Total Per Pupil Expenditures for Public Schools in US: Support Services - General Administration	29
$575	Total Per Pupil Expenditures for Public Schools in US: Support Services - School Administration	29
13,600	Number of Public School Districts in US	38
98,800	Number of Public Schools in the US	30
5,300	Number of Charter Schools in the US	30

---

38 http://nces.ed.gov/fastfacts/display.asp?id=372

Appendix IV: Educational Statistics

Figure	Metric	Footnote
33,400	Number of Private Schools in the US	30
$571,000,000,000	Estimated Total Expenditures for US Public Schools for 2012-2013 School Year	30
$11,467	Projected Expenditures per Student for US Public Schools for 2012-2013 School Year	30
49,828,000	Projected Enrollment in US Public Schools for 2012-2013 School Year	30
21,600,000	Number of Students Expected to Attend US Colleges and Universities in the Fall of 2012	30
$5,012,111	Average O&M Expenditures per School District	Calc
$1,081,304	Average Energy Expenditures per School District	Calc
1,104,888	Average square feet maintained per School District	Calc
124	Average acres maintained per School District	Calc

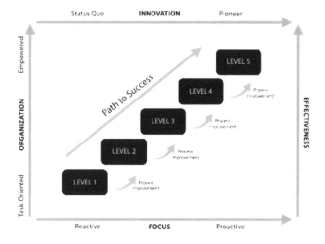

References

We offer the following references and resources as additional background information to support your implementation of the **OPM** at your school or institution.

1. APPA Facilities Performance Indicators Report,
   http://www.appa.org/research/fpi.cfm
2. Asset Management Maturity Model, Oarisk,
   http://www.oarisk.co.uk/Asset_Management_Maturity_Model.html
3. Balzer, William K (2010) Lean Higher Education: Increasing the Value and Performance of University Processes, Productivity Press, New York, NY
4. Barr, Stacey, *"The Performance Measure Specialist"*,
   http://www.staceybarr.com/
5. Bloodworth, Diane & Herron, David (2007) Developing Effective ITIL Key Performance Indicators,
   http://www.compaid.com/caiinternet/ezine/bloodworth-itil.pdf
6. Building Asset Performance Framework, A best practice guidelines for the performance assessment of Queensland Government buildings, Queensland Government, Department of Housing and Public Works, 2011
7. Campos, Marquez (2009) Review, Classification and Comparative Analysis of Maintenance Management Models,
   http://taylor.us.es/sim/documentos/resultados/JAMRIS_No03_20 09_P_110-115[1].pdf
8. Capability Maturity Model Integration (CMMI), Software Engineering Institute (Carnegie Mellon),
   http://www.sei.cmu.edu/library/abstracts/reports/10tr033.cfm
9. COBIT 5, ISACA,
   http://www.isaca.org/COBIT/Pages/default.aspx
10. Council of the Great City Schools – Performance Measurement and Benchmarking Project, http://www.cgcs.org/domain/86
11. Eckerson, Wayne W. (2006) Performance Dashboards: Measuring, Monitoring, and Managing Your Business, John Wiley & Sons, Hoboken, NJ
12. Education Criteria for Performance Excellence, Baldrige Performance Excellence Program, http://www.nist.gov/baldrige
13. EPA, Energy Efficiency in K-12 Schools,
    http://www.epa.gov/statelocalclimate/documents/pdf/k-12_guide.pdf

14. EPA, ENERGY STAR, Guidelines for Energy Management, http://www.energystar.gov/index.cfm?c=guidelines.guidelines_index
15. Facility Management Organization Maturity Model, http://www.iwmsnews.com/2009/03/the-fmo-maturity-model/
16. Fernandez, Marquez (2012) Maintenance Management in Network Utilities, Framework and Practical Implementation, Springer, London, England
17. Goldratt, Eliyahu M. (2004) The Goal: A Process for Ongoing Improvement, The North River Press, Great Barrington, MA
18. Google Data Center Efficiency, http://www.google.com/about/datacenters/efficiency/index.html
19. Google Green – Designing efficient data centers, http://www.google.com/green/efficiency/datacenters/
20. Imai, Masaaki (1986) Kaizen: The Key to Japan's Competitive Success, Random House, New York, NY
21. IT Information Library, http://www.itil-officialsite.com/
22. Joel Levitt (2008) Lean Maintenance, Industrial Press, New York, NY
23. Juran, J.M., (1964) Managerial Breakthrough: A new concept of the manager's job and a systematic approach to improvement management performance, McGraw-Hill, New York, NY
24. Humphrey, Watts S. (1989) Managing the Software Process, Addison-Wesley Publishing Company, Reading, MA
25. Kaplan, Robert S. & Norton, David P. (1996) The Balanced Scorecard: Translating Strategy into Action, Harvard Business School Publishing, Boston, MA
26. Kaplan, Robert S. & Norton, David P. (2000) The Strategy-Focused Organization: How Balanced Scorecard Companies Thrive in the New Business Environment, Harvard Business School Publishing, Boston, MA
27. Kaplan, Robert S. & Norton, David P. (2004) Strategy Maps: Converting Intangible Assets into Tangible Outcomes, Harvard Business School Publishing, Boston, MA
28. KPI Library, http://kpilibrary.com/categories/itsmitil
29. Liker, Jeffrey K (2004) The Toyota Way: 14 Management Principles from the World's Greatest Manufacturer, McGraw Hill, New York, NY
30. Madritsch, Thomas & Ebinger, Matthias (2011) "Performance Measurement in Facility Management – The Environment Management Maturity Model BEM3", Research Journal of Economics, Business and ICT, Volume 2, 2011, http://www.researchjournals.co.uk/documents/Vol2/web02.pdf

References

31. Maintenance Management Framework - Building Maintenance Policy, Standards and Strategy Development, Queensland Government, Department of Housing and Public Works, 2012
32. Managing for Results in America's Great City Schools, http://www.cgcs.org/cms/lib/DC00001581/Centricity/Domain/81/Managing%20for%20Results_2011.pdf
33. National Center for Education Statistics (2003) Planning Guide for Maintaining School Facilities, US Department of Education, Washington, DC, http://www.asbointl.org
34. Pierce, Sue (2011) *School Cents... The Energy Behavior Management Guide*, Sue Pierce, Cave Creek, AZ
35. Pourikas K. & Fitsilis, P. (2010) Applying Capability Maturity Model for Maintenance Services: A Case Study, http://www.logistics.teithe.gr/icsc2010/fullabstracts/7_4_ICSC2010_051_Pourikas_Fitsilis.pdf
36. Process Classification Framework for Education, APAC, http://www.apqc.org/knowledge-base/documents/apqc-process-classification-framework-pcf-education-pdf-version-201
37. Schneider, Mark (2002) Do School Facilities Affect Academic Outcomes?, National Clearinghouse for Educational Facilities, http://www.ncef.org/pubs/outcomes.pdf
38. Spain, Jack (2009) The IT Leadership Pyramid: Essential Leadership Imperatives for Leaders of Information Technology Organizations in the 21st Century, Spain Technovative Solutions, Cary, NC
39. Spain, Jack (2013) A Prescription for SMART Growth for Small to Mid-Size Businesses, Spain Technovative Solutions, Cary, NC
40. Strategic Asset Management Framework (SAMF), Department of Treasury, Government of Western Australia, http://www.treasury.wa.gov.au/cms/content.aspx?id=1269
41. the green grid – getting connect to efficient IT – Library and Tools, http://www.thegreengrid.org/library-and-tools.aspx
42. Wireman, Terry (2005) Developing Performance Indicators for Managing Maintenance, Industrial Press, New York, NY

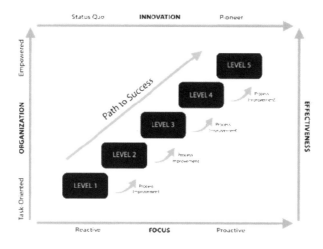

List of Figures

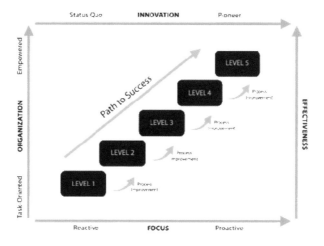

About the Author

Jack Spain support business development initiatives at SchoolDude. He has held executive and senior leadership roles in large corporations, mid-sized businesses, and small businesses for over 35 years. His professional experience includes key leadership roles in information technology, software development, marketing, business development, market research, and professional services organizations. His diverse industry experience includes manufacturing, transportation, energy, facilities and maintenance management, e-commerce, IT research and advisory services, technology commercialization, and executive recruiting.

He is a graduate of GE's Financial Management Program and holds a BA in Accounting and Economics from Edinboro University, has participated in executive education programs from Duke University, and has completed MBA coursework with Capella University. Spain has been a frequent speaker and presenter at industry events for several decades.

Jack published "A Prescription for SMART Growth for Small to Mid-Size Businesses"[39] in 2013 and "The IT Leadership Pyramid – Essential Leadership Imperatives for Leaders of Information Technology Organizations in the 21st Century in 2009.[40]

http://www.schooldude.com/opm
http://www.linkedin.com/in/jackspain

---

[39] http://www.SMARTGrowthSMB.com
[40] http://www.lulu.com/spotlight/SpainTechnovative

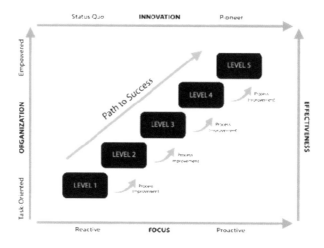

About SchoolDude

SchoolDude supplies software solutions for educational facilities and technology professionals and has served as the market leader in education enterprise asset management since 1999 with over 1 million education professionals using our platform. SchoolDude delivers cloud-based applications that help both small and large institutions better manage their facilities, IT, and business operations. We help clients save time and money by managing support services effectively and efficiently, allowing institutions to provide a safe teaching and learning environment. Today, we are the #1 provider of cloud solutions for public and private schools, colleges and universities.

http://www.schooldude.com/

TECHNOLOGY MANAGEMENT   MAINTENANCE MANAGEMENT

FACILITY USAGE

ENERGY MANAGEMENT

Made in the USA
Lexington, KY
13 October 2013